BROKEN TRUST

BROKEN TRUST

Overcoming an Intimate Betrayal

TIM COLE, PHD
EMILY DUDDLESTON, MA

Immēnsus Press
635 West Briar Place
Chicago, Illinois 60657
contact@immensuspress.com

ISBN 978-0-9983585-0-5 (Paperback)

First Edition

Publisher's Note: Throughout this book we use examples to highlight key ideas and illustrate effective communication skills. The couples presented in this book are not based on specific events or people; rather they were created to bring the research findings to life. This book is intended entirely for informational and educational purposes. Neither the publisher nor the author(s) hereby enters into any type of formal or informal legal, psychological, or professional relationship with any reader or purchaser of this book. Neither the publisher nor the author(s) are or will become liable to any such reader or purchaser for any legal or equitable claims or remedies of any kind, including, but not limited to, special, general, incidental, consequential, or other damages or any species of injunctive relief. Readers and purchasers of this book are solely and exclusively liable and responsible for their own risks, choices, decisions, actions, and outcomes with respect to how, why, and with whichever persons they make use of this book and its contents.

Cover by Michael Rehder
Interior design by Rachel Reiss

Contents

Acknowledgments

We're grateful for the help we received during the writing of this book. We are indebted to Jim Santor and Claudia Pitts for their feedback on early drafts of our work. We are appreciative of the editorial advice we received from the team of editors who helped us take our research and insights and turn them into a concise and practical guide to working through an intimate betrayal.

In particular, we would like to thank Joan Liebmann-Smith, Brooke Carey, and Patrick Price for their exceptional editorial input. We want to thank Terri Lonier for coming up with the title of our book and Edwind McGhee for developing a simple, jargon-free way of discussing attachment styles.

We are grateful for the feedback we received from hundreds of early readers who used our advice to work through an intimate betrayal. And we want to thank our families and friends for their patience and support.

BROKEN TRUST

Introduction

A partner's betrayal is one of the worst experiences you can endure. Depending on the severity of the betrayal, the loss of trust coupled with anger and hurt feelings can be overwhelming. Discovering a betrayal almost always brings out intense emotions such as loss, fear, sadness, shock, and disappointment. These feelings are to be expected when someone you love and trust behaves in a way that causes you harm. We want our partners to act with our best interests at heart, and when they fail to do so, we end up feeling devalued, rejected, and hurt—the consequences of broken trust.

Although you're going through a difficult time right now, we want to offer you some reassurance. Many relationships go through a major betrayal at some point in time, and if the situation is handled effectively, couples can not only recover from broken trust but actually grow closer and stronger in the process. In fact, research shows that even major betrayals such as infidelity are possible to overcome. If you approach the problem head-on and armed with the right knowledge and skills, you may find that you and your partner will come through this difficult time wiser and stronger and in a better place than before.

Perhaps you've discovered that your partner has been having an affair with someone from work. Or maybe you've discovered that your boyfriend has been in daily contact with his ex after promising to never talk to her again. Perhaps your fiancée failed to tell you about her bankruptcy, which prevented you from buying a house together. Or after twenty-five years of marriage, you find out that your husband is emotionally involved with someone else.

Intimate betrayals often come as a surprise, making them all the more difficult to manage. Take, for example, **Brian** and **Ashley**, who have been dating for three years and living together for the past year. Brian thought everything was great with their relationship, but then one day he received a Facebook message from a person he didn't know. The stranger claimed to be having an affair with Ashley and went into specifics about the different ways that he and Ashley had sex.

Brian had no idea what to make of the message. Was it some kind of sick joke? Was Ashley really cheating on him? Within seconds, he called Ashley and confronted her. Ashley denied his allegation, but Brian could tell by the sound of her voice that something wasn't right. After he got off the phone, he logged into Ashley's Facebook account and read the explicit messages between her and the other man. The proof of her betrayal turned his world upside down. Brian and Ashley were planning on getting engaged, and now those dreams were shattered. Brian was filled with so much anger, sadness, and disappointment that he was unable to think clearly. He was so distraught, he started to tear up and quickly made up an excuse to leave work in the middle of the day.

Of course, not all betrayals involve sexual infidelities. Take, for example, **Zachary** and his boyfriend **Jacob**, who have been in a long-distance relationship for two years. Zachary lives in New York City, and Jacob lives in Austin, Texas. For the past three months, Jacob has been trying to find a job on the East Coast, preferably in New York City, so he and Zachary can build a life together.

On a recent trip to Austin, Zachary was checking his email on Jacob's computer and discovered that Jacob had applied for several jobs in San Diego. Zachary had a hard time making sense of this information. Why would Jacob be applying for jobs in California? Zachary was stunned to find out that his partner had been making career choices that undermined their goal of creating a life together.

Betrayals are not only emotionally overwhelming, but they also create uncertainty, which leaves people asking basic questions about themselves ("Why didn't I see this coming?"), their partner ("How could he do this to me?"), and their relationship ("What does this mean for our future?"). Uncertainty robs people of their sense of security and peace of mind. It's difficult to know what to do when you begin to doubt the most basic things about yourself, your partner, and your relationship.

Betrayals are also stressful because the person you typically turn to for help and support is now the source of your anger and frustration. If you're like most people, you're struggling with some, if not all, of the following questions:

- How do I cope with my emotions?
- How can my partner and I break out of an endless series of confrontations and denials?
- How do I get my partner to tell me the truth and be less defensive?

- How can we begin to rebuild trust?
- How can my partner and I create a more loving and compassionate relationship?

If you're looking for the knowledge and skills needed to rebuild trust and repair your relationship, or if you want to come to terms with what you can realistically expect from your partner and learn how to bring out the best in their behavior, or if you just want some clarity and reassurance that moving on is the right thing to do, we wrote this book for you.

We have been through betrayals ourselves. More importantly, we have done research on the topic, taught classes on the subject, and helped thousands of couples work through their problems.

Tim has been studying issues of deception, betrayal, trust, and romantic relationships for decades. Our romantic relationships are incredibly complex—much more complex than even a calculus problem. They are also the most important connections we have. Nothing in life matters more than loving someone else and being loved in return. But being in love isn't easy. So many things can and do go wrong.

As it turns out, closeness and betrayal sometimes go hand in hand. You can only be betrayed by someone you trust, and typically that someone is the person you love the most. It's difficult to let someone get close to you without the possibility of being betrayed by that person at some point in time. When we're in love, we expect a lot from our partners and hold them to the highest of standards. Our partners, however, sometimes exercise poor judgment, make mistakes, and fall short of what's expected.

Simply put, our close relationships create incredible rewards, but they also come with some potential hidden costs that can catch us by surprise: heartache and betrayal. As Tim tells students, if you don't want to risk being betrayed, don't fall in love.

But going through life without love and intimacy completely misses the point of living in the first place. As social animals, humans need love and companionship in order to flourish. The key to having a fulfilling life is not to avoid close relationships and the betrayals that may occur. Sure, there are many ways you can prevent bad things from happening, but betrayals in a romantic relationship can never be completely ruled out. The secret to a successful relationship is learning how to deal with intimate betrayals constructively—in a way that brings people closer together, not further apart.

Our approach to dealing with an intimate betrayal is unique. We don't automatically assume that discovering a betrayal means that your relationship is damaged beyond repair. Our approach takes into account the reality that many relationships are faced with breaches of trust from time to time. There is no such thing as a perfect relationship—in other words, the idealized version of love and romance heavily promoted in our culture where partners who are truly in love never make mistakes or hurt each other.

In reality, our romantic relationships are sometimes difficult—complicated by contradictions and competing desires. Most of the time, our relationships bring us tremendous rewards—but not *all* of the time. Even the best romantic partners sometimes put their own desires and needs ahead of what is good for the relationship. Coming to terms with this reality helps people work through difficult problems as they arise. Creating a stronger, more successful relationship is possible when people accept that relationships require more than love. Most relationships encounter problems that eventually need to be addressed. True love requires working through such challenges as they emerge.

Our book is also unique in that we take your perspective as well as your partner's into account. The research on this is clear: both perspectives need to be addressed in order for there to be any reconciliation and forgiveness. While you definitely want your partner to understand the pain he or she has caused you, we know it can be difficult to see the situation from his or her point of view. However, if you want to recover from an intimate betrayal, you will eventually need to understand where your partner is coming from. What was your partner thinking, and what motivated their behavior? We will help you work through this process so that both you and your partner come to an agreed-upon meaning of exactly what happened. It's only through establishing a mutual understanding of how and why the betrayal occurred that relationships have the potential to grow closer and stronger.

We understand that it's important to address the emotional trauma you're going through. People are often reluctant to talk about being betrayed, generally out of misplaced feelings of shame or embarrassment. Far too many people struggle with an intimate betrayal on their own. While we provide a lot of knowledge and tools to help you cope with and express your emotions, we've also created a private online community (www.brokentrust.com) where you can share your experience and receive the help and support of others. Betrayals are easier to overcome when you can connect with people who understand exactly what you're going through.

Intimate Betrayal Defined

When most people think of an intimate betrayal, their minds immediately jump to one of the worst betrayals of all: infidelity. But the definition of betrayal encompasses a lot more. A betrayal "occurs when a social actor violates an established rule or expectation underlying cooperative behavior."

In terms of romantic relationships, a betrayal happens when a partner behaves in ways that go against your expectations—spoken or unspoken. All betrayals share this common structure (expectation + violation of that expectation = betrayal). Let's work through a trivial example. Imagine you don't want your partner to watch an episode of your favorite TV series without you (an expectation), but he secretly watches the episode and tries to hide it from you (a violation of your expectations). If you find out, you're likely to feel mildly disappointed (feel betrayed).

Major betrayals, like the one that led you to read this book, can include a wide range of issues such as cheating on someone, lying about one's identity, or concealing vital information (for example, a hidden bank account or a past drug problem). But betrayals can also include indiscretions like revealing a partner's confidential information to a third party, flirting with a colleague, or reading your girlfriend's email without her permission.

Here are the most common ways people betray their romantic partners:

- Lying about one's sexual history
- Infidelity and cheating

- Lying about past relationships
- Lying about flirting with others
- Concealing having strong feelings, interest, crushes, and attraction to others
- Secret contact with others
- Concealing drug use, alcohol abuse, or gambling problems
- Concealing debts and lying about spending habits
- Lying about feelings of love and commitment

In addition to a common structure (expectation + violation of that expectation = betrayal), all betrayals share one other thing in common: they all damage trust in your partner and the relationship. Trust is the belief that your partner will act with you and with your relationship's best interest in mind. It's hard to maintain trust when you discover your partner has acted on his or her own behalf at your expense.

Once trust begins to weaken, it typically sets off a chain reaction of accusations followed by more lies, deceptions, and betrayals, which increasingly erode what little trust remains. Because betrayals catch most people off guard, many individuals confront their partners in emotionally charged ways. Consider **Maria** and **George**, who had been married for fifteen years, were busy raising three young children, and owned one of the most popular restaurants in town. Like any other married couple, they had their share of ups and downs, but nothing serious presented itself until the day Maria learned that George had been having an affair with Teresa, one of their longtime employees. George had promised Teresa he would leave Maria when "the time was right." Teresa eventually realized the "right time" would never come and decided to tell Maria the truth about their affair. Of course, Maria reacted as most people would; she yelled and screamed at George in a fit of anger.

When confronted by a hostile partner, people tend to instinctively adopt a defensive position, which often causes them to cover their tracks by telling more lies. This is exactly what George did. Rather than come clean, he adamantly denied his affair, only digging himself deeper and doing more damage to his relationship. These counterproductive conversations, while common, ultimately make it more difficult for couples to work through a very difficult situation.

When a major betrayal occurs, the only way to prevent your relationship from deteriorating past the point of no return is by learning how to break out of counterproductive conversations, adopting new ways to address the issue, and taking steps to candidly discuss what happened.

It may seem counterintuitive, but there can actually be an upside to discovering a betrayal. Coming to terms with a betrayal provides the opportunity to identify and fix problems in your relationship. Problems are always going to arise in any relationship. Learning how to deal with problems in ways that restore trust and foster intimacy can lead to a deeper sense of love and commitment. And by learning how to address issues as they arise, you will be better able to deal with future problems before they turn into a full-blown crisis.

How Our Advice Is Presented

To help you work through the betrayal you've encountered, we've organized our book into two parts. In the first half of the book, we help you make sense of *why* and *how* you were betrayed and provide some guidelines for assessing the damage done. We also help you decide if your relationship is worth trying to save. Next, we identify common relational problems that underlie most intimate transgressions. We also provide insight into the different ways that people react to an intimate betrayal.

In the second half of the book, we provide the skills and knowledge you need to help you manage your emotions. We also offer detailed advice and techniques to repair broken trust and help you create a healthier and more satisfying relationship. We know you may be tempted to jump to the second half of the book because you're undoubtedly looking for solutions, but you'll have a better chance of success if you fully understand the dynamics underlying an intimate betrayal before applying the skills needed to make things better.

As we offer a way forward, we identify and discuss many pitfalls that couples fall into when trying to work through an intimate betrayal. You may have already encountered some of these pitfalls as you tried to work things out with your partner. As we point out these common pitfalls, the important thing is not to get hung up on what didn't work, but to use those experiences and examples as a reference point for trying new techniques. And you don't have to be perfect when following our advice—it's not even possible to be perfect, especially in a time of crisis. If you slip up and fall back into old habits or counterproductive behaviors, as you become aware that you're doing so, cut yourself some slack, take a moment to regroup, and approach the problem with the skills and techniques provided in the chapters to come.

We include a lot of activities in the second half of the book designed to help you work through the betrayal you experienced. While some of the activities are fairly simple, they will provide you with real benefits. You may be tempted to skip them because you think you get the point we are trying to make. Please don't do this. Only by doing the activities will you bring about the desired results.

And as mentioned, we've created a website for you, the readers of our book. This website (www.brokentrust. com) is a private, confidential online community where you can share your experiences, ask us questions, and get advice from us and others on how best to move forward, given your particular circumstances. This online community includes assessment tools, online journals, forums, and a variety of additional resources to help you cope with and recover from an intimate betrayal.

We know you're probably dealing with a lot of issues right now, so we've tried to keep our advice simple, brief, and to the point. We're confident our approach will help you work through the betrayal you've encountered and give you the tools you need to strengthen and repair your relationship.

PART I

Understanding Betrayals and the Dynamics of Your Relationship

CHAPTER 1

The Paradox of Intimacy

YOU'RE PROBABLY ASKING, "Why did this happen to me?" Although you're undoubtedly hurting right now, it may help to know that many people experience a betrayal at some point in their romantic relationships—you're definitely not alone. And although common, betrayals still take most people by surprise—few people expect a romantic partner to betray their trust. Because people don't anticipate being betrayed, most people aren't equipped to deal with the aftermath.

When you're forced to deal with situations with little warning or preparation, it's common to look for someone or something to blame. This is especially the case when one has been betrayed by a romantic partner—it's so easy to blame a partner for the harm they've caused. Sometimes people even blame themselves for being betrayed ("There must be something wrong with me"). And in many cases, people automatically assume that their relationship is fundamentally flawed.

But what if you were able to look at the situation from a different perspective? What if you were able to take a step back for a moment and look at the problem as something that happens to many people at some point or another? What if the betrayal isn't a reflection on you or your partner's character, love, or devotion? What if the problem is simply due to an aspect of our romantic relationships that we tend to overlook? That is, what if betrayals tend to go hand in hand with our relationships, and we have biases that make it hard for us to acknowledge this reality. We place a ton of expectations on our romantic partners. Sooner or later people are likely to mess up. It's probably not realistic to expect someone to always live up to your expectations.

The Paradox of Intimacy

To understand why your partner betrayed your trust, it helps to grasp one of the most important and universal truths about our romantic relationships: that even in the most ideal circumstances, relationships are incredibly complex and difficult to manage. In fact, making a romantic relationship work is one of the most challenging tasks you will ever do. The idea that relationships are difficult to manage—that love creates both rewards and constraints—is what we call the "Paradox of Intimacy." Learning how to reconcile this paradox is the key to effectively understanding and dealing with an intimate betrayal.

So what exactly is the Paradox of Intimacy? It's the idea that being close to someone else always carries some risk. Falling in love creates a competing set of dynamics. While intimacy creates many positive outcomes, these rewards are not cost-free; intimacy also has a downside. When people become intimately involved with someone, they inevitably give up some of their personal freedoms. But before we get to that, let's look at the benefits of the Paradox of Intimacy.

Being in love not only feels fantastic, it also fundamentally changes the way we experience life. Research consistently shows that people in loving relationships live longer, healthier, and happier lives than those who aren't. Even mundane activities—such as walking the dog, listening to music, or simply eating dinner—are much more fun when shared with a romantic partner.

Being in a loving relationship also helps us cope with life's ups and downs. Scientists have found that individuals who are part of a loving, healthy relationship weather stressful life events, such as a job loss or serious illness, better than those who aren't. It's difficult to overstate the benefits that love creates.

Of course, as anyone who has been in a relationship knows, getting close to a partner also presents certain challenges. As relationships become more intimate, we place an increasing amount of expectations on our partners. And the closer we get to someone, the more our choices and actions impact our partner's choices and actions, and vice versa. When we fall in love, we go from being *independent* to becoming *interdependent*—no longer free to do what we want, when we want, and with whom we want—because any decisions we make not only affect ourselves but our partners as well.

Lauren and **Mike** had been dating seriously for about nine months when they decided to move in together. Things had been going great. Like most couples, they'd enjoyed getting to know each other, taking short trips together, and meeting each other's family and friends. Everything had been new, exciting, and fun, and since they were spending practically every night together and got along so well, moving in together made sense. Plus, it would help them each save on rent.

That's when this new relationship got complicated. Mike soon realized he hardly had any time to himself, and he couldn't have his friends over without first checking with Lauren. Suddenly Mike had to get up earlier in the morning because Lauren expected him to drive her to work. On top of that, Lauren's family insisted on everyone getting together for dinner every Friday—Mike included. Over time, Mike is learning that living with Lauren means giving up some of his autonomy.

Lauren, too, felt she was giving up a lot. She felt she didn't have enough time to focus on her work as a freelance graphic designer because Mike wanted her to be home when he got off work and expected her to attend sporting events together during the week. Lauren also felt pressured to spend time with Mike's friends and was frustrated that she had to check with Mike before making plans of her own. They both were starting to feel the constraints, as well as the joys, of intimacy.

For the most part, people try to live up to their partner's expectations and want to make their partner happy. But it's not possible for *anyone* to please a romantic partner all of the time. You and your partner will disagree on almost anything at one time or another—such as financial decisions, how to spend the holidays, how and when to have sex, whom to socialize with, and how to raise kids—among many, many other things.

There are several practical reasons why partners cannot always live up to each other's expectations. To

Common Examples of Unrealistic Expectations and Beliefs

- Relationships should be based on the complete truth.
- Partners should share everything with each other including thoughts, feelings, and beliefs.
- Disagreements and conflicts are detrimental to relationships.
- Romantic relationships should always be full of desire and passion.
- Sexual desire should be exclusive; one should never have sexual feelings or thoughts for someone else.

begin with, we tend to place some unrealistic expectations on our partners, our relationships, and love in general. Unrealistic expectations stem from the very act of falling in love. Love is a powerful emotion, which causes many people to view their partners in idealistic but unrealistic ways. For example, when people fall in love, they often assume that they should understand each other completely, that they should even know what the other person is thinking without having to say a word, that love should be based on complete intimacy, and that couples should create a joint identity and downplay or even completely forgo their individual identities.

When couples set unrealistic expectations about their romantic relationships, they put tremendous pressure on their partners. Most people want their partner's approval but find they struggle to live up to such unrealistic demands.

Think about it for a minute. People struggle to live up to their own expectations on a daily basis. Parents struggle to be patient with their kids; friends struggle to withhold criticism; and neighbors struggle to be civil with each other. People struggle to manage their finances, their weight, and their time in general. If we can't meet our own expectations, is it realistic to hold our partners to a higher standard? No, and yet we do it all the time. We want our romantic partners to live up to our expectations because it makes us feel safe, loved, and valued.

Not only do partners struggle to meet unrealistic expectations; people also struggle with competing demands. Although romantic partners place expectations on each other, people have to deal with others' expectations as well. Life would be easier if people only had to be concerned about pleasing their partners. But, in the real world, dealing with competing expectations is a fact of life. For example, you may be looking forward to enjoying a long weekend with your partner; however one of his kids from a previous relationship is going through a bad breakup and needs his help—throwing a wrench into your weekend plans.

And sometimes, people put their own needs ahead of their partner's expectations. People often experience competing desires, and most of the time, when these competing desires arise, people try to do the right thing. However, no one is perfect. Sometimes decent, caring people exercise poor judgment and put their own needs ahead of what's best for the relationship.

Lauren, for example, remained close with her ex, Ryan, after she and Mike started dating. Although Lauren and Ryan couldn't make their relationship work, they still enjoyed each other's company and considered themselves friends. Lauren would talk to Mike about Ryan, and it upset Mike because he didn't think it was appropriate for her to remain friends with an ex. In fact, Mike became so upset, he raised his voice and told Lauren that he wanted her to stop talking to Ryan altogether. Because Lauren loved Mike, she took his perspective into account and tried to avoid doing things with her ex. However, one day Ryan stopped by Lauren's work unannounced and offered to take her out for lunch. Lauren went to lunch with Ryan because she wanted to catch up with her friend.

Not only do people sometimes fail to live up to their partner's expectations, but under certain circumstances, people often conceal what they've done. People sometimes conceal the truth because they are ashamed of their own behavior, or they want to avoid punishment, or they don't want to hurt their partner's feelings, or they simply don't want to have a long, dragged-out conversation about the issue. For example, when Lauren occasionally sees Ryan, she conceals it from Mike because she feels bad about what she's done; she doesn't want to hurt Mike's feelings; and she doesn't want to spend hours talking about the issue with him.

When people fear that the truth might lead to a negative outcome, especially a partner's disapproval and even punishment, telling the truth becomes a less attractive option. *Fear* is a powerful emotion—fear of hurting a partner's feelings, fear of getting into trouble, and fear of damaging a relationship.

Although we all value honesty, research on deception in close relationships shows that deceiving a partner is an innate response designed to keep us on good terms with our partners. Omitting the truth sometimes helps people avoid conflict, hurting each other's feelings, and

Deceptive Communication

Tim teaches a course on deceptive communication, and as part of that course, he has his students keep a journal on their deceptive behavior. After every conversation they have throughout their day, his students are asked to reflect on whether they told the truth. Before starting this exercise, most students are unaware of the extent of their deceptive behavior. While doing this assignment, his students are surprised at how often they lie and how easy it is to do. Tim's students' experiences are consistent with published research findings: when telling the truth is likely to result in hurting someone's feelings, disapproval, or other negative reactions, concealment, for the most part, is an automatic, natural response.

getting drawn into time-consuming conversations. We aren't saying that misleading a partner is the right thing to do, but it happens more often than we think.

Deceptive behavior begins early in life; children as young as three years old begin lying in order to avoid some type of disapproval. For example, in one study children were seated in a room full of toys that were hidden from their view. The children were warned not to look at the toys, but when they were left alone for a few minutes, they, of course, took a peek. When later asked if they had done so, most of them lied. Not only did they lie, but they were really good at fooling others, including their parents.

In fact, misleading others comes so naturally that most people don't realize they're doing it. Most lies, whether big or little, are not rehearsed or planned; they happen on the spur of the moment—an automatic, reflexive response.

Piecing Together the Paradox

When you consider all the dynamics described above, the paradox becomes clear: Honesty is essential to a romantic relationship because it allows partners to grow close. But this closeness brings with it many expectations and constraints—expectations that partners sometimes struggle to meet. Ironically, it's the fear of disappointing a partner that ultimately leads to a betrayal of trust.

Our romantic relationships are incredibly complex because of this paradox, and this dynamic plays itself out in countless ways. Partners share their lives with each other, but they may also conceal their latest shopping spree, their flirtatious behavior at work, or the fact that they are attracted to someone else.

It's only when a betrayal comes to light that people become aware of the Paradox of Intimacy and immediately question if their relationship is broken beyond repair. Sure there might be a few lucky individuals who are never exposed to a partner's betrayal, but for the most part, many people experience the hurt, anger, and confusion from discovering broken promises and deception in their romantic relationships.

Using the Paradox of Intimacy to Solve Problems More Effectively

It would be great, of course, if we could create relationships where partners *always* live up to each other's expectations and *never* lie. But that's not the world we live in. We can, however, use our knowledge about the Paradox of Intimacy to solve problems in our relationships more effectively.

The secret to working through an intimate betrayal is learning how to communicate with a partner in a way that promotes closeness and understanding, but doesn't make a partner feel threatened when telling the truth. We know that learning such skills can be difficult, but they are critical when trying to deal with an intimate betrayal.

We're not saying that the skills laid out in this book will solve all of your relational problems, but they'll help you resolve issues of broken trust in the most effective way possible. If you can't deal with the problems in your relationship using the techniques we provide, then that can be an indication of more serious problems, and you might want to consider consulting a therapist or marriage counselor. Or it might be an indication that the issues in your relationship can't be reconciled; ending a relationship is sometimes the best thing to do.

Four Principles When Dealing with Broken Trust

The Paradox of Intimacy reveals four interrelated principles about dealing with broken trust:

- Focus on expectations
- Honor your emotions
- Focus on the big picture
- Communicate constructively

Focus on Expectations. When you understand that all breaches of trust involve a violation of your expectations,

Common Relational Expectations

To help you reflect on the expectations you might hold about your partner and vice versa, here's a list of commonly held expectations people place on their romantic partners:

- Be faithful.
- Be honest and reliable.
- Be flexible, understanding, and considerate.
- Be affectionate and have fulfilling and frequent (or infrequent!) sex.
- Put me and our relationship first.
- Remember birthdays, anniversaries, and other important dates.
- Be supportive in a time of need.
- Be positive and fun to be around.

focusing on the specific expectation at hand not only helps clarify what's going on but also helps shift the focus back to more productive ground. It can help guide the conversation back to your wants and needs and away from your anger, disappointment, or frustration. When you focus on your expectations, you can address the real problem: Your partner isn't meeting your needs, which is causing you to question your value, your partner's value, or the value of the relationship itself.

For example, Zachary immediately got angry with Jacob for applying for jobs on the West Coast and focused his anger on how Jacob betrayed his trust. However, if Zachary had instead focused on his expectations—that he's looking for someone to build a future with—it would have helped him frame the betrayal in terms of the real issue at stake: Zachary wants Jacob to make their relationship his top priority.

Honor Your Emotions. Broken trust creates strong emotional reactions. When we experience intense, negative feelings, we naturally want to feel better, and one way to make our negative feelings go away is to pass them on to someone else—usually the person whose actions triggered our feelings—by yelling, screaming, and attacking them. While attacking a partner may provide some temporary emotional relief, it doesn't solve the problem and can, in fact, exacerbate it. The Paradox of Intimacy reveals that when people express their emotions in hostile and aggressive ways, they foster less openness and honesty in their relationships. In fact, attacking or criticizing a partner ultimately creates a defensive environment where you can count on more lies being told. On the other hand, dismissing your emotions or letting them get the better of you will not help you understand why you were betrayed nor lead to a meaningful resolution of the problem.

In order to deal effectively with your emotions, you must acknowledge and honor them. Your feelings are legitimate; don't let your partner or other people discount them. Our feelings are designed to alert us to opportunities and problems. When you've been betrayed, use your feelings to identify the expectations your partner violated. Take that emotional energy and focus on the specific ways you want to be treated in your relationship. Using your emotions this way will help you work through the betrayal you encountered while avoiding damage to yourself and your relationship.

In the second half of this book, we provide detailed advice on how to best use your emotions rather than letting your emotions get the best of you.

Focus on the Big Picture. When you've been betrayed, it's wise to take a moment to reflect on the big picture. What's your ultimate goal? Do you want your partner to acknowledge the pain they've caused? Do you want to know what truly happened? Do you want to try to work toward some type of resolution? When people don't focus on their goals, it's easy to let their immediate emotional concerns get in the way—like trying to punish a partner or make them suffer. Acting on such immediate feelings often makes it more difficult to accomplish your larger objectives.

For example, when Maria discovered George had been cheating on her, she didn't consider what she hoped to accomplish. Rather than think about what she wanted from George, she acted on her impulses and yelled and screamed at George for hours on end. When people don't reflect on the big picture and what they ultimately hope to achieve, their actions lack focus and can lead to unwanted outcomes. Did Maria want to chew George out? Vent her anger? Get her husband to apologize? When people don't have a clear goal in mind, it's nearly impossible to arrive at a satisfying outcome.

Communicate Constructively. When people discover they have been betrayed, there can be societal pressure to kick a partner to the curb. People are often told that they have to stick it to their partner—otherwise they will come across as being weak and will be taken advantage of again. However, the Paradox of Intimacy—the realization that our relationships are full of competing demands, desires, and wishes—highlights the importance of dealing with the betrayal by adopting a constructive approach.

The only possible way you and your partner can repair the damage done is by discussing the issue without hostility and defensiveness. It's only by creating a mutual understanding of what happened that you will be able to achieve reconciliation. We know it's not easy to adopt a constructive approach when you're hurting. In fact, acting in anger and ending a relationship is often the simple and easy way out. Trying to work through a betrayal with a partner in a constructive way actually takes a lot of strength and perseverance.

A constructive approach happens when couples realize that they are on the same side—that it's "us versus the problem" not "you versus me." Relationships are a team effort. At some point or another, couples experience hurt feelings, disappointment, anger, and resentment. When negative things happen in your relationship, if you can take a step back and approach your partner with a cooperative, constructive mind-set, you'll discover that it's a better way to deal with problems as they arise.

Imagine if Mike had been able to explain his concerns about Lauren spending time with her ex, rather than blowing up at her. And imagine if Lauren had been able to explain where she was coming from—she didn't ever want to hurt Mike's feelings, but she also valued her friendship with Ryan. By talking about the issue candidly, an agreed-upon understanding might have been reached. Perhaps they would have agreed that Lauren could spend time with Ryan as long as Mike was included.

But even when couples can't arrive at a solution, by adopting a constructive mind-set, couples can talk about problems in ways that demonstrate concern and respect for each other, even when disagreements arise. Feeling valued and respected, especially when problems emerge, serves as the foundation for having a healthy and successful relationship. Everyone wants to feel understood, valued, and cared for. So how couples talk about problems makes all the difference in the world.

When couples don't deal with problems using a constructive approach they're likely to keep encountering them. Learning how to deal with problems constructively also makes it easier to see when partners aren't truly motivated to resolve issues—like when a partner refuses to empathize with the pain and distress he or she caused. If you approach your partner constructively, and he or she doesn't show concern, that can be very revealing.

We know it can be unsettling to view romantic relationships as a paradox. And we know that it's difficult for some people to accept that their romantic relationship may never live up to an idealistic Hollywood version of true love. But we also know that coming to terms with the Paradox of Intimacy helps people communicate in ways that create a more genuine relationship. When you feel confident approaching your partner constructively, you may find that you spend less time worrying about problems and more time enjoying your relationship.

Putting It All Together

Managing a close relationship is one of the most difficult things you can do. Intimate relationships bring joy, happiness, and meaning to our lives, but they are also full of contradictions and potential heartache. Understanding how this paradox works can help alleviate feelings of uncertainty and confusion. Knowing about the Paradox of Intimacy also highlights the importance of identifying your expectations, honoring your emotions, focusing on your goals, and adopting a constructive approach when relational problems come to light.

Takeaways

- Intimacy creates tremendous rewards in a romantic relationship.
- Intimacy also places many constraints on each partner.
- The Paradox of Intimacy occasionally leads people to betray or deceive a partner.
- When dealing with an intimate betrayal, it's important to identify your expectations, honor your emotions, reflect on the big picture, and try to address the issue constructively.

CHAPTER 2

Is Your Relationship Worth Saving?

WHEN YOU'VE BEEN betrayed, it's very difficult to evaluate the situation with a clear head. In this chapter, we'll offer some practical guidelines to help you figure out the damage that's been done. Sometimes, no matter how hard you try, a partner's betrayal can damage a relationship beyond repair, and moving on is the smartest thing to do.

There are several good reasons why a relationship should come to an end. If the betrayal involved physical or emotional abuse—your partner hit, pushed, or threatened to harm you—or this betrayal is another in a series that has become a pattern of betrayals, the relationship is probably not worth saving. You may also want to consider ending a relationship if the betrayal you experienced stems from a serious flaw in your partner's personality—a flaw where he or she cannot empathize with you or take your feelings or well-being into account. Additionally, when a partner commits a severe transgression, a deal breaker, which not only devalues your relationship but also changes the way you see yourself, it may be time to reevaluate whether you want to try to work things out.

We also provide you with some advice for evaluating the quality of your relationship. If your relationship wasn't rewarding before the discovery occurred, it may not be in your best interest to work through the betrayal you encountered. Having an assessment of both the damage done as well as the strengths and weaknesses of your relationship can help you make the best decision on how to proceed.

Again, most romantic betrayals are caused by relational dynamics—the Paradox of Intimacy. However, if you're involved with someone who has a serious problem taking your needs into account and being considerate—and they repeatedly deceive you (and others)—then the advice in this book will be of little help. Some individuals have personality traits, known as the Dark Triad, where they consistently take advantage of others in their interpersonal relationships. Additionally, a partner who has a borderline personality may also have difficulty acting in ways that are considerate and respectful.

Dark Triad

Pathological Narcissism. People with a narcissistic personality can be quite charming and attractive at first. They can rope you in with their ability to tell a good story and make you feel important. With that said, these people are incredibly self-absorbed, egotistical, and selfish. They only want you in their life so you can play the role of the adoring spectator. They need your compliments, attention, and focus, but they will never care about you as much as they care about themselves. Due to their lack of empathy and their sense of entitlement, they are bound to betray a partner's trust; the normal rules of decency, honesty, and faithfulness (among other traits) simply don't apply to them.

To add insult to injury, dealing with *their* mistakes is nearly impossible because *they* don't make mistakes! *You* do! It's difficult for narcissistic individuals to take ownership of anything negative that happens in their lives. As such, solving problems with narcissistic partners can be challenging. Again, some questions to consider:

Does your partner—
- lack empathy?
- constantly seek out prestige and status?
- take advantage of you and others?
- demand excessive amounts of attention?
- have an inflated sense of self-importance?
- expect special treatment from you and others?

If you answer yes to most of these questions, your partner may have a narcissistic personality.

Machiavellian Personality. People with a Machiavellian personality take a cold, manipulative approach to their romantic relationships. They can be very flattering but use their charm to exploit their partners for their own gain. They consistently put their needs ahead of others', using both hard tactics (threats, deception, manipulation) as well as soft ones (charm and flattery) to get their way. Their goal is not to help you achieve your goals, but to trick you into helping them get ahead with little to no concern for your well-being. Here are some questions you should ask yourself if you're concerned that your partner might have a Machiavellian personality:

Does your partner—
- seem emotionally aloof?
- exploit others for his or her gain?
- use lies and deception to get ahead?
- manipulate others to get what he or she wants?
- use flattery and charm to accomplish his or her goals?
- put his or her needs and goals ahead of everyone else's?

If you answer yes to most of these questions, it's an indication that your partner may have a Machiavellian personality.

Psychopathic Personality. Having a relationship with a partner who has a psychopathic personality can be much more difficult than having a partner who is narcissistic or Machiavellian. People with psychopathic personalities like to take risks and have little, if any, concern about the damage they do to you and others. Watch out! They're incredibly reckless and can be emotionally or even physically dangerous. Betrayal is a way of life for them. Look for a long line of victims in their past, which they will probably try to hide from you. It's virtually impossible to have a meaningful long-term relationship with someone who has a psychopathic personality.

Does your partner—
- hold an overly cynical view of relationships?
- use deception to take advantage of others?
- show a lack of guilt or remorse for their behavior?
- ignore social norms and have little concern for right or wrong?
- exhibit shallow emotions and tend to be cold-hearted and insensitive?
- act impulsively with little regard for the safety of themselves or others?

If you answer yes to most of these questions, your partner might have a psychopathic personality.

Borderline Personality

Partners who suffer from borderline personality can also cause serious concerns. Borderline individuals can be easy to connect with—they're often exciting and can be lots of fun—but they have some fairly significant drawbacks. Among others, they are *terrified* of being abandoned. Their own terror of not being loved can cause them to freak out and engage in extreme behaviors: One minute everything is great; you're the most incredible person in the world. And the next it's utter chaos because they don't feel important and loved, and you're now the worst person they've ever run across.

Small, trivial events can trigger an extreme reaction. If you don't show up on time, or don't respond to their text messages right away, or you cancel plans at the last minute, you may encounter a fierce and unreasonable response from a partner with a borderline personality.

In addition, they often act out in very controlling ways, lack empathy and self-restraint, and may panic at times when a calm and rational response would come in handy. When it comes to dealing with a partner with a borderline personality, you can count on this: they will often push your buttons and violate your expectations. Here are some questions you should ask yourself if you're concerned that your partner might have a borderline personality:

> Does your partner—
> - engage in self-destructive, impulsive behavior (such as sex, drugs, shopping sprees, or reckless driving)?
> - frantically try to avoid being left out or abandoned?
> - have intense mood swings?
> - fly into inappropriate fits of anger and rage?
> - experience problems in their interpersonal relationships?
> - switch between thinking you're the best and worst person in the world?

If you answer yes to most of these questions, your partner may have a borderline personality.

If you suspect your partner might have a dark or borderline personality, seek professional help for yourself and your partner, if he or she is willing. The advice we offer in this book isn't going to work when a partner's behavior stems from a significant shortcoming in his or her personality. You're dealing with a much larger problem than a string of broken promises; you're dealing with someone who does not consistently care about your needs, feelings, or even physical safety and might

Important Note

Determining if your partner may have one or more of the personality traits listed above can be tricky. Many people have some of the listed characteristics, and personality traits can overlap, resulting in a diverse array of symptoms. An evaluation by a mental health professional is needed to make a proper diagnosis. There are also several online tests, which can be used to assess personality type (see the *Broken Trust* website for links to the most current online assessments).

therefore be dangerous. That's why it's essential you seek professional help as soon as possible.

Deal Breakers

Some betrayals are definitely deal breakers. Most people find it next to impossible to trust a partner after experiencing serial infidelity, financial fabrications or fraud, sexual scandals, and other very serious transgressions. Such betrayals not only devalue your relationship but also threaten your identity or self-image and are difficult to recover from. For example, if you discover your partner is leading a double life—he or she has another family on the side—it not only shows disrespect for you, but it can change the way you see yourself. Suddenly you've unknowingly become a participant in a three-way relationship, or perhaps you now also see yourself as a fool—a person who lacks judgment and awareness of what's going on in the most intimate part of your life. When a betrayal changes a fundamental aspect of your identity, the path to recovery can be extremely challenging.

Severity of the Damage

If the betrayal you're dealing with is not quite a deal breaker but involves the breach of a very important expectation, trust in your partner will have been damaged, and you'll have a lot of work ahead of you. Again, most betrayals damage relationships, not break them. When a major betrayal occurs, it helps to know exactly how much damage has been done. Consider several factors to help you evaluate the amount of work you have ahead of you.

How Discovered? How you discovered the betrayal matters. If your partner came to you and confessed because he or she was feeling guilty, that's a good sign. Genuinely re-morseful partners truly want to make things right; they come forward because they are motivated to fix the problems they caused. It's easier to work through an intimate betrayal with a truly remorseful partner.

However, when a partner confesses because his or her hand was forced, it's less than ideal—it's difficult to trust someone who is not forthcoming. For example, did your partner tell you about the transgression right before it was going to come to light anyway? If so, you'll have more work to do to reestablish trust because you'll probably question your partner's motives, with good reason. Was your partner just trying to save his or her hide rather than acting with your best interest in mind?

If your partner had no intention of telling the truth, and you discovered the transgression on your own, you can still save your relationship, but you will have a lot of work ahead of you. It can be difficult to regain trust when your partner actively hid the truth from you. In fact, if that's what happened, it's natural to start questioning what else your partner may be hiding.

Going back to our couples, both Maria and Brian found out through a third party that their partners were cheating on them. George had been having an affair for about a year and had no intention of ending it before he got caught. Ashley had no intention of telling Brian about her infidelity, and he moved out because he didn't feel he could trust her. And Jacob completely hid the fact he was looking for jobs on the West Coast from his partner. His transgression only came to light by accident. More time and effort is required to fix a betrayal that was discovered by chance.

Pattern or Onetime Incident? Onetime betrayals are typically easier to deal with than repeated ones. Recurring transgressions most likely indicate a disparity between what you want from a partner (your expectations) and what he or she is truly able to do. In other words, recurring problems won't be easily resolved. For example, when Maria got to the bottom of the truth, she discovered George had been involved with multiple women for at least five years. Likewise, Jacob had been hiding many issues from Zachary, including his feelings of love for his partner and his level of commitment to the relationship.

Discovering a recurring betrayal may indicate that you and your partner may not be compatible on some, if not many, fundamental levels. Recurring issues also suggest that you and your partner don't have the skills necessary to work through the problem (hence, they continue). If you can't resolve the problem when it first occurs, it will most likely be repeated and continue to damage your relationship, unless you adopt new ways of dealing with it.

This was the first time Ashley cheated on Brian, so while Ashley's infidelity was a major transgression, at least it didn't represent a pattern of behavior, and it should be easier for them to get their relationship back on track.

State of Your Relationship

If you were already unhappy in your relationship before you discovered the betrayal, that's not a good sign. Recovering from an intimate betrayal requires a lot of motivation and commitment. If your relationship wasn't rewarding before you discovered your partner's transgression, what's the point?

Maria loved her life before she discovered George's affair. She loved her husband, her children, and the business they built together, and she was extremely happy. Likewise, Brian was extremely happy with Ashley before he discovered her cheating. She brought much excitement and happiness into his life, and he thought she was amazing. In both these relationships there is a strong motivation to work through the betrayal. In the case of Zachary and Jacob, Zachary is constantly frustrated by the lack of attention he receives from his boyfriend. When relationships aren't built on a solid foundation, the betrayal often reveals larger issues that have been simmering for a while. Here are more guidelines to help you determine if your relationship is on solid or shaky ground.

Lack of Shared Vision. Many couples are simply incompatible—they do not belong together. Relationships are partnerships in which two individuals work together to achieve their mutual goals. If you and your partner are not on the same page about what you want out of life or what you want your relationship to be, no amount of love can overcome this obstacle. For example, if you want to focus on your career, and raising a family isn't of interest to you, but your partner really wants kids, no amount of love or compromise can help you resolve that difference. You're going to experience more of the negative side (heartache and disappointment) than the positive side of the Paradox of Intimacy. If you're involved with someone who doesn't share your values and goals, your relationship will actually be an obstacle to your personal happiness and success.

Lack of Motivation and Skills. You should also consider ending a relationship when a partner lacks the motivation to make things better or the skills to do so. Many people say they want to change but lack the motivation to follow through. A partner can easily say, "I'm sorry" and "I promise to change," but talk is cheap. Action is the real deal. When it comes to betrayals, our best advice is to ignore what your partner says and watch what he or she actually does. It's only through carefully observing a partner's behavior that we learn the truth about his or her motivation.

Or put another way, because intimate betrayals are common, it's not whether mistakes were made or not; what truly matters is what happens *after* the fact. A partner who cares for you learns from his or her mistakes and takes action to prevent it from happening again. When a partner doesn't show this type of concern or motivation, that's a huge red flag. There is little, if any, point in being in a relationship with someone who isn't interested in making sure that you're happy.

It's also possible to end up in a situation where you're involved with someone who *is* motivated to make things better, but they just don't know how to do so. For example, your partner may have difficulty directly sharing or communicating his or her feelings or talking about problems in your relationship. If your partner's intentions align with yours, and he or she is just *unaware* of how to get things back on track, the advice provided in this book is designed to help.

Guidelines for Evaluating a Relationship

It ultimately comes down to this: Are you in a healthy relationship in which problems emerge from time to time? Or are you in a relationship that is more of a grind than a reward? We provide some criteria in the following fifteen-question assessment to help you figure out if your relationship is worth saving—or if it's best to move on.

Relationships are meant to add value to your life. People who are in a healthy relationship receive physical, emotional, and financial security. Successful couples enjoy better health outcomes and live longer than others. They're also happier and feel more confident with their place in life. If your relationship is causing you health problems or is a constant source of anger, frustration, anxiety, and sleepless nights, it's probably time to have an honest conversation with your partner—and yourself.

To evaluate the state of your relationship prior to the betrayal that occurred, it helps to answer these questions.

We have created an online version of this assessment tool as well.

1. If I had to create a short list of two or three people with whom I could spend the day, my partner would be on that list.

   AGREE ___   DISAGREE ___

2. My partner and I laugh a lot together.

   AGREE ___   DISAGREE ___

3. My partner and I have the same values, goals, and interests.

   AGREE ___   DISAGREE ___

4. My partner and I get a lot of enjoyment out of doing the same activities together.

   AGREE ___   DISAGREE ___

5. My partner expresses the amount of love, affection, and appreciation that I need.

   AGREE ___   DISAGREE ___

6. My partner is attentive to my needs.

   AGREE ___   DISAGREE ___

7. My partner does not show a lot of hostility, disregard, and contempt for me, especially when we disagree.

   AGREE ___   DISAGREE ___

8. My partner makes me feel understood.

   AGREE ___   DISAGREE ___

9. When having a discussion, my partner listens to what I have to say.

   AGREE ___   DISAGREE ___

10. My partner views me as an equal and treats me with respect.

AGREE __   DISAGREE __

11. My partner doesn't make me feel used, exploited, or taken for granted.

AGREE __   DISAGREE __

12. I know that my partner will be there for me in a time of crisis.

AGREE __   DISAGREE __

13. I feel comfortable sharing my innermost thoughts and feelings with my partner.

AGREE __   DISAGREE __

14. When it comes to household tasks, or other things that need to get done, there is a strong sense of shared responsibility.

AGREE __   DISAGREE __

15. My partner satisfies me sexually.

AGREE __   DISAGREE __

Now give yourself 1 point for each question you generally agree with before the betrayal came to light.

TOTAL SCORE _____

If you score 12 points or more, your relationship (outside of the betrayal) is in good shape. It's probably wise to focus on the issue that led you to read this book and implement the advice we provide on how to fix your relationship.

If you scored somewhere between 7 and 11 points, you definitely have some issues to explore. Take a close look at the questions you didn't agree with—those are issues that are going to cause problems in your relationship. Are the issues you identified the ones both you and your partner are motivated to work through? And do you both have the skills necessary to do so? Again, the advice in this book is designed to help such couples. And working with a therapist may also be in your best interest.

Anything below 7 indicates that it's time to seriously consider what you're getting out of the relationship. While you may have strong feelings for your partner, don't confuse feelings of love with a healthy relationship. Healthy relationships require more than just love. Healthy relationships are partnerships based on mutual respect, concern, and support. Only healthy relationships provide the benefits everyone wants—joy and happiness, and all the riches they create.

Additional Issues to Consider

Think about all of the rewards you get out of your relationship, whatever they may be (for example, companionship, love, and financial stability, among others). Compare those rewards with all of the costs you encounter in your relationship (such as heartache, disappointment, frustration, or loneliness). When you compare the rewards of your relationship to the costs, do you come out ahead? And is your relationship, as a whole, better than you thought it would be? If not, can you clearly identify the problems? Do you think they can be resolved? Unresolved issues put a great deal of stress on a relationship. Being in a highly strained relationship is only going to lead to more misery.

It also helps to consider your alternatives. If you weren't in your relationship, what would you be doing? Would you be better off on your own? Can you envision creating a better life with someone else? Staying with a partner solely because you can't envision a better future without your partner is not a wise reason to stick it out. If you're not happy, and you've done your best to improve your relationship, don't let your lack of options or fear of loneliness hold you back from leaving an unhealthy relationship.

Research shows that people who leave problematic relationships are better off in the long run. If you don't like your alternatives, take small steps to improve the options you do have. The best way to do this is to take care of yourself in the present, as well as do things that are in your best long-term interest. Perhaps this involves getting in better physical shape, learning new skills, trying new hobbies, or meeting new people. Anything you can do to improve yourself will enhance your options in life. And people with options are better at assessing the true value of their relationships.

Finally, do you feel that you've invested too much in your relationship to let it end? If you've spent years or decades with someone, it can be hard to evaluate your relationship clearly. When people make such large investments, it clouds their judgment. You have probably heard the saying, "Don't throw good money after bad money." The same sentiment applies to your relationship: *Don't throw away your future by trying to fix a broken past.* While it can be difficult to walk away from a relationship, sometimes it's in your best interest. If you already feel as if you've spent too much time in a bad relationship, why let yourself spend more?

At the end of the day, only you can make the final assessment about your relationship; you're the one who has to live with the consequences as well as your partner. If you think it's time to call it quits, there are many factors to consider, including legal, financial, your emotional and physical safety, and the welfare of children, just to name a few. If you do decide it's in your best interest to break things off, talk to both a therapist and an attorney about the best way to end your relationship, given your specific circumstances.

Putting It All Together

Sometimes discovering a betrayal reveals more than an issue that needs to be addressed. If your partner has a dark personality, commits a deal-breaking transgression, or hurts you beyond repair, or your relationship wasn't satisfying to begin with, then ending a relationship is probably in your best interest.

Your happiness in life depends on the quality of your relationships. If you're not in a meaningful and satisfying relationship, it'll be difficult to lead a fulfilling life. However, if you're struggling with a major betrayal in an otherwise loving and healthy relationship, the advice in this book is designed to help you repair the damage that's been done.

Takeaways

- If your partner has a dark personality, it's probably time to call the relationship quits.

- Sometimes the damage done by a betrayal is beyond repair.
- The quality of your relationship prior to the discovery of a betrayal is one of the most important factors to consider.
- If your partner lacks the motivation to solve inevitable problems in your relationship, it will be difficult to lead a fulfilling life together.

CHAPTER 3

How We Attach

B EING BETRAYED FORCES people to grapple with questions about their partners and their relationships. Research consistently shows that discovering a betrayal also leads to a great deal of self-reflection. Self-reflection is most helpful when people develop a greater understanding of the issues underlying the betrayal that occurred. Increased self-awareness can help couples avoid common pitfalls and patterns of communication, which are counterproductive when trying to discuss the problem with your partner. Developing greater insight into how you and your partner relate to each other will also make it easier for you to implement the advice we provide throughout the second part of this book.

People who lack self-awareness of their motivations and needs, when it comes to intimacy, are likely to encounter the same relational problems over and over again with little insight into what's going on. To avoid repeating mistakes and falling into traps when talking to your partner about what happened, it's essential to understand the differences in how you and your partner experience intimacy.

When we talk about self-awareness, most people think about the differences between the sexes. They assume that men and women are vastly different from each other when it comes to relationships—that they hold different expectations and experience intimacy in different ways. Although we have a tendency to view men and women as being fundamentally different from each other, research doesn't reflect this.

In terms of relationships, men and women are more similar to each other than they are different. There is, however, one difference that most people are not aware of that provides critical insights into how people set expectations, express their emotions, experience empathy, and attempt to deal with an intimate betrayal, and it's not based on gender. Rather, it's the difference in attachment styles each partner brings to the relationship.

Understanding Your Style of Attachment

People don't experience intimacy in exactly the same way. In fact, there are four different *styles of attachment*—ways that people relate to their partners when it comes to love and intimacy. Understanding your and your partner's styles of attachment will help you make sense of every aspect of the transgression you're going through. It will also help explain the dynamics of your relationship and highlight the specific issues you will face as a couple when trying to recover from an intimate betrayal.

There are two ways you can find out your attachment style. One is through our website: www.brokentrust.com.

When you have the time, we strongly recommend using the interactive Attachment Style Test on our site; it provides a very accurate assessment of how you interact with your partner. But if you want to jump in right now, take our quick Attachment Style Quiz that follows here. Read each scenario and choose the response that best describes how you would behave in such a situation. Don't overthink your choice; just go with your gut reaction.

"Last Night Out" Scenario

Imagine that, after dating your partner for several years, you've finally decided to get married. You both decide to have one last night out with your same-sex friends before the wedding—the standard bachelor and bachelorette parties. You and your fiancé aren't living together, so you promise to call each other when you get in.

Both of you are planning on a late evening, but you promise to make that call no matter how late. After a long night of fun, you call your fiancé on your way home at around 4:00 a.m. Your call goes to voice-mail, so you send a text message instead. You head home and (select a response).

RESPONSE A: *You're getting ready for bed. You think about your fiancé and hope he or she is having a lot of fun. You may feel like trying to touch base one more time, but you're also tired and ready to crash for the night.*

RESPONSE B: *You call your partner again and again and again. Although part of you thinks every-*

thing is probably OK, part of you is feeling anxious about getting in touch with him or her. You check your phone repeatedly, calling and texting from time to time. You have a hard time falling asleep—you just really want to know what's going on. You're concerned; until you hear from your fiancé, your worries may get the best of you.

RESPONSE C: *You get home and don't think twice that your fiancé has not checked in yet. You're crashing for the night and know that you'll hear from him or her eventually.*

RESPONSE D: *You get home and you're feeling anxious and confused. Part of you is questioning why your fiancé didn't answer your call, but part of you didn't really want to talk anyway. You're relieved and irritated at the same time.*

Back to the Scenario

Your fiancé finally calls you early the next morning and (select a response).

RESPONSE A: *You're happy to hear from your fiancé and are interested in finding out how the evening went.*

RESPONSE B: *You're furious! You've been up all night worried that something was wrong. You have a hard time controlling your feelings and let your anger come out by asking pointed questions, "Why didn't you call me?" "What were you* really *doing?" Or you may try to pretend that everything is fine, but on the inside you're frustrated, hurt, and disappointed. You may even give your partner the silent treatment.*

RESPONSE C: *You're somewhat peeved because your fiancé called so early in the morning. You don't feel like talking, so you say, "Can I call you back later?"*

RESPONSE D: *You aren't sure how you will react. You might be really upset or totally disinterested. Your feelings change quickly from moment to moment.*

If you selected response A in both scenarios, you have a **confident style** of attachment.

If you selected response B in both, you have a **concerned style** of attachment.

If you selected response C in both, you have a **cool style** of attachment.

If you selected response D in both, you have a **confused style** of attachment.

If you have mixed results, you have a combination of more than one style of attachment; you fall somewhere in between two different styles of attachment, which is common. It's also important to highlight that attachment styles vary in terms of their intensity. Perhaps you're mildly concerned, moderately confident, or strongly cool. Taking the attachment test provided online will give you a more detailed assessment of where your attachment style falls.

Attachment styles are formed through early childhood experiences and can be modified based on major life events (such as parental divorce or major illness), positive and negative experiences in significant romantic relationships (including the betrayal you're experiencing), as well as meditation and therapy.

The next step is to go over the scenarios and responses again and try to guess how your partner will respond. Then apply the evaluations above to see what his or her style of attachment might be. Based on your and your partner's attachment styles, intimate betrayals play out in very predictable ways. We'll cover specific attachment style pairings in the next chapter.

Right now, it will help you to become familiar with the different styles of attachment. If you have a mixed style of attachment (for example, confident-concerned or confident-cool), that simply means you have aspects of two styles of attachment, and you fall somewhere in between.

Confident Style of Attachment

Those with a confident style of attachment are very comfortable with intimacy. They aren't afraid of making commitments or letting partners get close. They're trusting and tend to look for the best in other people, especially in their romantic partners. At the same time, confident individuals understand that everyone needs some degree of privacy and autonomy, even in a romantic relationship. People who have a confident style of attachment are good at managing the Paradox of Intimacy. They value both closeness *and* autonomy and can share their lives with their partners without losing sight of their individual needs and concerns. Confident individuals know their partners don't want to spend every minute of their time with them or share everything that happens, and that's OK.

People with a confident style also understand that relationships aren't perfect—all relationships come with problems, which constantly need to be addressed. But they know that relationships are worth all of the effort because nothing in life is more important than being loved and loving someone in return. Because of their positive outlook on relationships, confident people approach relationship problems constructively—in ways that show a great deal of consideration and respect for their partners. When really upset, confident individuals may act out but quickly shift to a constructive approach—knowing that it's important to try to work through the issue by being thoughtful and considerate.

People often develop a confident style of attachment based on how they were treated as babies, in childhood, and in most of their romantic relationships. If you were consistently treated with love and concern, but allowed to explore and make mistakes by parents, then you probably have a confident style of attachment. Essentially, confident people feel secure. They know they can take care of themselves, but they also know that others, especially their partners, can be counted on.

When it comes to dealing with an intimate betrayal, those with a confident style of attachment have an easier time than others acknowledging their emotions and thinking about how to best solve problems with their partners. It's relatively easy for confident individuals to identify their expectations and discuss them with their partners. Although they can be overwhelmed by their emotions from time to time and occasionally explode, confident individuals are quick to regroup, focus on their goals, and engage their partners constructively.

Confident individuals are also good when it comes to being considerate and understanding. They can easily see situations from both their own and their partner's point of view. And they also try hard to live up to their partner's expectations and feel genuine remorse if they happen to be the one to betray their partner's trust.

If both you *and* your partner have a confident style of attachment, you probably will be able to express your emotions clearly, listen to each other respectfully, and work together to overcome the transgression that occurred. However, if only one of you has a confident style of attachment, depending on who that person is—the betrayed or betrayer—different obstacles lie ahead.

This was the situation with Maria, who has a confident style of attachment, and her husband, George. Maria completely put her trust in George, who has a cool style of attachment (see below), and expected the best from him. So when she found out that he cheated on her, she was furious not only because he had an affair, but also because of how he responded—he lied to her and then completely "checked out." While Maria wanted to understand why George cheated on her, he didn't want to talk about what had happened; he just wanted to put the past in the past and move on.

Despite her initial outburst, Maria was eventually able to regain her bearings, focus on her goals, and express herself as best she could. Maria's confident style of attachment came through when she told her husband, "I'm so hurt right now, the only thing that will get me through this is knowing the truth, however painful it might be.

Can we focus on this issue right now? I really want to understand what's going on with you."

Concerned Style of Attachment

For people with a concerned attachment style, their hearts are in the right place—they deeply value and cherish their relationships. Such individuals greatly desire intimacy in their relationships, often to the point where they downplay the importance of their own needs and goals. Their relationships always come first. They sometimes have a difficult time allowing their partners to have a separate identity. In terms of the Paradox of Intimacy, concerned individuals stress the importance of intimacy and are uncomfortable with the idea that individuals still have needs, interests, and goals that fall outside the bounds of the relationship.

When Lauren and Mike began dating, she dropped out of her Saturday morning running group so she could spend time with him. After they had been dating for a while, she started to miss her running friends and their Saturday morning routine—a long run followed by a lengthy, boisterous brunch. When Lauren rejoined the group, Mike expressed interest in joining as well. But she told him that it was something she wanted to do on her own.

Mike, who has a concerned style of attachment, was extremely hurt. He didn't understand why she'd want to do something without him. Mike felt betrayed and started to question if Lauren really cared about him. By comparison, someone with a more confident style of attachment might feel excluded as well, but they are more likely to understand that partners sometimes need time to themselves and tend not to let such incidents lead to doubts about the relationship.

For concerned individuals, the focus on closeness and intimacy in their relationships is driven by concerns over their sense of self-worth. They have a deep-seated fear of being abandoned. They love their partners and desperately want to be loved, but are worried that their romantic partners won't love them as much in return. In fact, they often fear that their partners will leave them for someone else. They hope their partners will be good to them, but they secretly (and sometimes not so secretly) question if their partners truly love them.

Due to these fears, individuals with a concerned style of attachment tend to be preoccupied with their relationships. They focus on their romantic partners and spend much of their time thinking about them. They always want more closeness in their relationships and become easily frustrated when that doesn't happen.

For example, even before Zachary discovered that Jacob was looking for a job in California that would make being together more difficult, Zachary often thought that Jacob might leave him. So when Jacob shows any signs of disinterest—like not responding to his phone calls or canceling plans at the last minute—Zachary has a difficult time coping. Initially, he tries to pretend that everything is OK. He doesn't want to upset his boyfriend with his whining. But eventually his feelings get the best of him, and he freaks out. He yells, screams, and confronts Jacob in a burst of anger asking him, "How could you treat me like this? Why don't you care about me?"

People usually develop a concerned style of attachment because of the care they received as babies. Concerned attachment can be caused when parents are inconsistent in the care they give to their children. When parents show concern one moment and are indifferent the next, babies feel uncertain about themselves and their ability to be loved and cared for, and they become overly preoccupied with their parents.

Concerned attachment can also be caused when parents are overly protective (helicopter parents) and don't let their very young children make mistakes, explore, and take minor risks (such as walking without holding someone's hand). Such children learn they have much less power than their more powerful parents.

In short, when children don't feel safe or aren't given the freedom to explore, they become fixated on their parents' love and approval. While attachment styles develop in early childhood, they usually carry throughout life, but in some cases, major negative life events or poor treatment in an important romantic relationship can cause confident people to adopt a concerned style of attachment. For the most part, concerned individuals are looking for stronger and wiser partners who (they hope) will provide them with a greater sense of love and safety.

When it comes to betrayals, people who have a concerned style of attachment tend to place more unrealistic expectations on their partners without always being aware of what they're doing. It's understandable that individuals who don't feel safe would lean on partners and want their partners to do the most to make them feel secure. While they place many demands on a partner, they can have a difficult time expressing their expectations. They're often afraid that their partners will leave them if they make their wishes clear, perhaps because they overwhelmed previous partners with their demands.

Ironically, because they try to sweep many issues under the rug, they can suddenly have explosive reactions when frustrated or when a significant betrayal comes to light.

Concerned individuals are also prone to explosive reactions because they question how much they are cared for. So when a partner does something to make them feel devalued, their worst fears spring to life. Their emotions get the best of them, and they often act on their feelings without considering the consequences. They often overidentify with their emotions because, deep down, they don't expect their partners to be attentive to their concerns. In many situations, they end up exaggerating their emotions and distress, hoping that it will get their partners to give them the attention and love they desire. When they are upset, their primary goal is to feel safe, not necessarily to resolve the issue with a partner. Typically, they make demands and try to control a partner's behavior in an unconscious attempt to alleviate their distress—like Zachary does when he explodes because Jacob isn't as attentive as he would like him to be. Concerned individuals' lack of security can get in the way of their honoring their emotions and approaching problems constructively.

Anxious, overly concerned people also try hard to live up to their partner's expectations, but then get angry when their partner doesn't seem to make the same effort. As such, they may betray a partner's trust to get attention or love from someone else, or get even with their partner for not loving them enough.

When confronted with their behavior, they're likely to deny what happened, or beg for forgiveness and make promises never to betray their partner again. Concerned people tend to have a hard time empathizing with their partner because their feelings of inadequacy and the intensity of their own emotions make it difficult for them to put their own point of view aside for a few moments and take their partner's feelings into account.

If you or your partner has a concerned style of attachment, your hearts are in the right place; you are motivated to make your relationship work. With the right knowledge and skills, concerned individuals can learn how to work through an intimate betrayal.

Cool Style of Attachment

While some people have a lot of anxiety about love and intimacy, others tend to be more indifferent and less engaged in their romantic relationships. At a very deep, unconscious level, they're reluctant to let a partner get too close. Such people have a cool style of attachment. They fear commitment and can come across as being aloof, cold, and distant when issues involving intimacy and closeness arise in their romantic relationships. Those with a cool style of attachment stress the need for individuality over their desire to connect with a partner. In terms of the Paradox of Intimacy, cool individuals value their autonomy more than intimacy.

Cool individuals like to keep a lot of emotional distance between themselves and their partners. They become very uncomfortable when lovers try to get too close, become too attached, or become overly dependent (like when a relationship starts to get serious). Making commitments and following through is not their strong suit. They need a lot of space in their relationships, or they will start to emotionally "check out."

As such, cool partners would rather avoid activities that create intimacy such as kissing, talking about their feelings, or doing things that couples are "supposed" to do. George, as we said earlier, has a cool style of attachment. While he likes the stability of his relationship and loves his children, he isn't comfortable opening up with his emotions—they make him feel too vulnerable, so he tends to ignore how he's feeling.

People with a cool style of attachment are more likely than others to end up in situations where they are intimately involved with several people. They are more likely to play games when it comes to love. By being involved in multiple relationships, cool individuals ironically maintain a sense of autonomy—*I'm my own person. I don't belong to anyone.* Having several superficial, "intimate" relationships helps them maintain their distance from everyone.

Like George, Jacob also has a cool style of attachment. He likes being in a relationship with Zachary, but it's not the most important thing in his life. He loves spending time with his friends and sometimes feels trapped in his relationship with his boyfriend. Jacob finds relationships to be overly constraining, so he acts in ways that create some distance from Zachary, like sometimes ignoring Zachary's text messages and phone calls. Cool partners want to have a relationship while trying to avoid the intimacy and commitment it requires.

Those with a cool style of attachment often grew up in environments where their needs were not consistently met. At an early age, they learned to dismiss or downplay their needs because their feelings and concerns were not attended to. Essentially, they try their best to take care of themselves above all others because they believe that no one else will.

When it comes to intimate betrayals, people who have a cool style of attachment often don't give much thought to what they expect from their partners, much less what their partners expect from them. But when they notice that one of their expectations has been violated, they aren't surprised—they *know* that others shouldn't be trusted. They're likely to deal with betrayals (their own or their partner's) in a dismissive manner, ignoring the problem or often preferring to walk away from a relationship rather than trying to work things out.

Cool individuals don't like to explore their own emotions, let alone address what their partners are going through. However, when pushed to their breaking point, their emotions can briefly erupt in violent outbursts in which they are likely to utter hurtful, relationship-ending comments: "I hate you! I'm done! Get out of my life!"

Individuals with a cool style of attachment are also most likely to betray their partner's trust. Cool individuals are unlikely to be concerned about living up to a partner's expectations. They tend to value their autonomy more than their partner's approval, so when confronted with their transgressions, they tend to shut down or attack back (both techniques succeed in pushing partners away). If you or your partner has a cool style of attachment, rebuilding trust is going to take a lot of effort. Again, later in this book, we provide you with the knowledge and skills that can help.

Confused Style of Attachment

People with a confused style of attachment experience more difficulties in their relationships. Confused partners tend to be all over the place. Like concerned partners, they desperately want to be loved. However, they're also like cool individuals in that they dislike it when people get too close. In terms of the Paradox of Intimacy, they struggle to make sense of their strong and conflicting needs for autonomy and closeness.

As such, confused individuals are constantly acting inconsistently—they draw people in, only to push them away. Dating someone with a confused style of attachment can be like riding an emotional roller coaster. They can be emotionally volatile—they can act in ways that are simultaneously needy and aloof, concerned and distant, nice and nasty, and so on.

Unfortunately, people with a confused style of attachment don't understand their own needs and reactions, making it difficult for them to talk about what they're experiencing. For the most part, confused individuals usually have short-lived romantic relationships because their emotions are so inconsistent and unpredictable.

Those who develop a confused style of attachment were typically raised in households where there was a lot of hostility, anger, and abuse (emotional and/or physical). If you have a confused style of attachment, our best advice is to seek counseling. And if you think your partner might have a confused style of attachment, you might consider going to therapy together. In either case, trying to deal with this problem without professional help can be extremely challenging.

Throughout the rest of this book, we aren't able to offer a lot of specific advice for people with a confused attachment style. Because they can exhibit both cool and concerned tendencies, confused individuals often act inconsistently from moment to moment or may even freeze up—their conflicting emotions can sometimes leave them in a state of indecision. Again, working with a therapist is often helpful for people with a confused attachment style.

Attachment and Romantic Relationships

To understand how you and your partner may have gotten into the situations you're in, it helps to understand how romantic relationships are formed. How you form a romantic relationship is similar to how you bonded with your parent as a baby. Babies form a strong attachment to the person who provides the closest physical contact— skin-to-skin contact, baby talk, prolonged eye contact, kissing, cuddling, and caressing, among other types of intimate contact.

For better or worse, adults use the same signals when forming attachments in romantic relationships. People form romantic attachments to the person with whom they have the closest physical contact. This may help explain why some couples engage in "baby talk" as adults; it's one of the ways people form attachments.

It's also important to know that attraction, love, and attachment are three separate dynamics. Attraction is based on physical arousal; love is based on emotional intimacy; and attachment is based on security and comfort. You can be attracted to many people, fall in love with someone you're not attracted to physically, and be attached to someone you no longer love.

For instance, while many relationships start out based on physical attraction, they don't have to. Sometimes people just "click" despite a lack of physical attraction;

they find each other more interesting, entertaining, and engaging than sexually appealing. But then they may decide to spend more time getting to know each other, which can create feelings of closeness and intimacy. Whether relationships start based on physical attraction or feelings of connection, love and repeated sexual contact often follow.

Unfortunately, love can blind people from reality as an attachment between two people starts to form. When people fall in love, they become somewhat delusional and tend to overlook a partner's flaws and believe their relationship is unique and unlikely to run into problems. They also want to spend a lot of time with their partner, which usually involves having a lot of sex. All of that physical contact (kissing, cuddling, caressing) triggers the attachment system. Eventually, people become attached to each other. Just like a baby seeks out his or her parent or caregiver in a time of distress, adults turn to their attachment figures in times of crisis.

Attachments are just like security blankets; they provide people with a sense of stability and calm. Almost everyone is capable of forming an attachment; people just do it in different ways, as we have seen.

Simply put, lovers become each other's adult caregivers. Attachment styles simply reflect the different types of attention people need and expect from their romantic partners.

Again, most of the time the process works like this: attraction leads to involvement, which can lead to passionate love, which results in an attachment-based relationship. Passionate, intense sexual love is short-lived (two to four years). At that point, passionate love may turn into companionate love (you *truly* like each other and love being together), a loveless relationship, or an enduring attachment to someone you dislike.

Once an attachment forms, it can be very difficult to break, even if your partner is breaking your heart or you don't like them very much. In fact, breaking an attachment creates loss—one of life's most stressful and painful experiences. That's why it's always a good idea to get to know someone before you become physically involved with him or her; doing so can save you a lot of heartache in the long run. While this advice may come too late for some, perhaps it can help in future relationships.

An individual's attachment style is not always obvious at first. It can be difficult to discern someone's individual style of attachment based on everyday, casual interaction. In fact, research shows that both cool and concerned people present themselves differently than their true style of attachment would suggest. When first dating, a concerned person's anxiety often comes across as "high energy," quirky, playful, and charismatic. Cool people, on the other hand, may come across as being warm and genuine. Why? They likely aren't intentionally misleading you, but attachment styles really come to life when an actual attachment is formed. It's easy to be playful and fun until the relationship becomes serious and one's fear of abandonment surfaces. Likewise, it's easy to act warm and genuine in a casual context. A cool individual's fear of intimacy may not rear its head until the relationship becomes a "real thing."

The bottom line is you don't necessarily see your partner's style of attachment until it's too late. Or put more bluntly, the person you marry is not the person you divorce.

Also, everyone is on their best behavior when dating. Think of all the time people spend picking out just the right outfit, all the polite and kind things they do and say to each other, and even the genuine excitement that comes across in the tone of their voice on the first few dates.

Sadly, as time passes, such endearing behaviors begin to disappear, or at least become more sporadic. According to research, as couples become closer, they become curter and meaner to each other—much meaner than they would be to a complete stranger. Think about that for a minute.

Many people form expectations for a relationship based on faulty first impressions. Coupled with the fact that love clouds one's judgment, it's easy to see why people often form relationships in which their attachment needs are not aligned with their partner's needs. It's a perfect storm: hidden attachment styles, everyone putting their best face forward, and both believing the relationship is rosier than it actually is. Is it any wonder that so many romantic relationships fail? Falling in love turns out to be much easier than falling for the right person.

Comparing Attachment Styles

Confident Partners tend to be trusting of others, good at managing their emotions, and willing to take their partner's perspective into account when trying to solve problems.

They're—
• the least likely to betray their partners.

- the most likely to deal with the discovery of a betrayal constructively, trying to talk it out with their partner rather than getting overly emotional or shut down.
- the most likely to show remorse and work to mend the relationship when they betray a partner's trust.

Concerned Partners tend to worry about being loved, often let their emotions get the best of them, and are more likely to punish or try to control their partner when problems emerge.

They're—
- more likely to betray their partner than confident individuals.
- more likely to disregard minor issues until a moderate-to-severe betrayal occurs, or enough small transgressions break the camel's back, after which an explosive reaction is likely.
- the most likely to experience shame, act defensively, or make hasty promises to change when they betray their partner.
- more likely to be highly motivated to work through problems in their relationships.

Cool Partners tend to distrust their partner, downplay their emotions, and put less effort into dealing with problems in their relationships.

They're—
- the most likely to betray a partner and keep secrets.
- the most likely to call it quits when a partner's betrayal comes to light.

- more likely to become irritated, minimize the issue, or blame their partner for what happened when confronted about betraying a partner's trust.
- more likely to give their partner a lot of freedom.

Putting It All Together

It helps to view betrayals through the lens of attachment because understanding both parties' attachment styles explains a lot about how intimate betrayals play out in a romantic relationship. People with a confident style of attachment are good at honoring their emotions, setting goals, and working through problems constructively. Those with a concerned style of interaction tend to overidentify with their emotions. They don't act in ways that attempt to address the problem but rather attempt to make their feelings go away—usually by controlling their partners. Cool individuals dismiss or deny their emotions and have little motivation for working through an intimate betrayal.

It's also important to keep in mind that the different attachment styles apply to both men and women; there are concerned men and cool women. Don't let stereotypes about gender cloud your thinking about intimate betrayal; attachment styles are often more informative and influential than sex differences.

Throughout the rest of this book, we'll be using your and your partner's style of attachment to help explain how to work through an intimate betrayal.

Takeaways

- You and your partner each have a specific style of attachment.
- Your attachment style influences the expectations you set, the emotions you feel, and how you express yourself.
- Your and your partner's style of attachment largely influences how betrayals play out.

CHAPTER 4

How You Match

L ET'S TAKE A deeper look at some of the complications and challenges people face as they work through a relational transgression within specific attachment style pairings. If you're still overwhelmed by the betrayal you experienced, it may be helpful to only read the section that applies to your relationship's specific pairing as well as the last section of this chapter, which explains why couples stay in relationships even when their attachment styles clash. You can always come back later and read this entire chapter.

Confident-Confident Pairing

Two confidently attached individuals have a much easier time than others at working through all types of problems in their relationship, including the discovery of a major betrayal. Those with confident styles of attachment

Confident Partner *Betrays* Confident Partner Motivation for Betrayal	Confident Partner *Betrayed by* Confident Partner Reaction to Betrayal
Finds it difficult to always meet partner's expectations—the Paradox of Intimacy. "Life is full of competing demands and sometimes I put my own interests ahead of the relationship. I'm not perfect, I make mistakes."	Feeling disappointed, hurt, and sad, but depending on the circumstances, confident people are more likely than others to express their emotions, engage in perspective taking, and find mutually agreed-upon solutions to resolve their relationship problems. "Everyone messes up, let's try to figure this out."

tend to be good at understanding their emotions, taking their partner's perspectives into account, and dealing with issues that arise in their relationship using constructive communication skills. Essentially, when relational problems emerge, two confidently attached people are more likely to adopt an attitude of "us versus the problem we are facing" rather than a "you versus me" mentality.

Consider **Nathan** (confident) and **Addison** (confident), a couple who have been together for three years and just recently got married. They enjoy each other's company and share many interests, including the way they met—through their love of adventure travel. Now that they are married, they are excited to start the next phase of their lives together. Of course, like all couples, they've encountered some growing pains—building a life with someone is never easy.

Right now, the main sticking point in their relationship is Addison's sister, Haley. Haley is somewhat irresponsible and has a hard time keeping a job. Before they got married, Addison would send her sister money when she was down on her luck, which was often. But since sharing their finances, Nathan isn't comfortable supporting Haley financially. He thinks that giving her money prevents her from taking responsibility for her life. He also wants to travel the world with Addison before they start their family, and the extra money could come in handy.

Although Addison agrees with her husband in theory, she has a hard time turning her back on her sister (competing expectations). Recently, she gave Haley money and tried to hide it from him. Of course, the truth came out. While Nathan was extremely upset, he and his wife were able to share their feelings, understand each other's point of view, and find a solution to prevent it from happening again. They set up a joint financial account so she and her husband would manage their finances together. The next time her sister came to her seeking money, there was literally no way Addison could give her money without involving her husband in the discussion.

Two people with a confident style of attachment have an easier time reaping the rewards that intimacy and closeness provide, and they can more quickly overcome the many challenges and obstacles that emerge. Like Nathan and Addison, when a transgression occurs, they quickly find a way to work together, understand each other's point of view, resolve the breach of trust, and turn their attention back to enjoying their relationship.

If you and your partner both have a confident style of attachment, the advice provided in this book will be easier for you to implement. But if one of you doesn't have a confident style (see additional pairings), the road ahead will be more difficult, but not impossible. In the chapters to come, we'll provide you with the knowledge and skills needed to communicate more effectively with your partner.

Confident-Concerned Pairings

Confident Partner *Betrays* **Concerned Partner** **Motivation for Betrayal**	**Concerned Partner** *Betrayed by* **Confident Partner** **Reaction to Betrayal**
The Paradox of Intimacy and the need to sometimes rebel against a concerned partner's needy behavior. "I sometimes feel overwhelmed by the demands placed on me in this relationship, and I act out because I feel like I'm losing control over my life."	Feels frightened and sad. Wants to do anything to save the relationship. Might try to sweep small transgressions under the rug until that strategy doesn't work. A moderate-to-severe betrayal may trigger intense feelings of insecurity. Likely to engage in an explosive reaction and controlling style of communication. "How could you do this to me?! Stop it! I need you to…"

Confident Partner *Betrays* Concerned Partner

When confident people betray their concerned partner's trust, it's often because they feel as if their concerned partners are being too controlling and taking over too many aspects or details of their lives. Consider another couple, **Josh** (concerned) and **Liz** (confident), who met their freshmen year of college and have been dating for over a year. Because of their similar school and work schedules, they spend a lot of time together. When they are not together, Josh feels the need to reach out to Liz. While Liz appreciates the attention, she sometimes feels as if she is overly constrained by Josh's need to be in constant contact. The only time Liz feels like she doesn't have to respond to Josh is when she is at work. Occasionally, she simply wants some time to herself, so she tells Josh she has to work, when, in fact, she has the day off. She could tell him the truth, but it probably would not go over very well. Josh reacts poorly when she tells him that she needs some space. Instead of hurting his feelings, Liz has found that it's easier to bend the truth.

If you have a confident style of attachment and you're sometimes betraying your partner's trust because of their concerned style of attachment, there are better ways to address your need for autonomy. There are ways to explain your need for some independence that are less likely to trigger your partner's fear of abandonment.

Concerned Partner *Betrayed by* Confident Partner

When concerned people discover that their confident partner has betrayed them, it can create waves of doubt and insecurity. Their own emotional reactions often get in the way of their trying to make things better.

Anxiety makes it difficult for people to express their emotions, focus on their goals, and approach their partners constructively.

Eventually, Liz got caught lying to Josh about being at work. One day he decided to visit her at the restaurant where she waitressed, only to find out she wasn't even on the schedule that day. He flipped out. Instead of taking a moment to pause and reflect, he acted on his worst fear—Liz was trying to leave him. He was going to get to the bottom of what was going on. He checked with all of their mutual friends, trying to figure out where she was and what she was doing. When Liz heard from one of their friends that Josh was looking for her, she was overcome by dread. She knew it wasn't going to be easy to explain why she had lied to him.

When Josh and Liz finally talked, it didn't go well. He demanded to know where she had been and to see her cell phone. He also wanted all of her logins and passwords. Although Josh just wanted to feel safe, he didn't realize that by making demands rather than expressing his feelings, he was pushing Liz further away. He was unknowingly highlighting the constraints of intimacy, rather than working toward creating its benefits.

If you have a concerned style of attachment and were betrayed by a partner with a confident attachment style, it may be difficult for you to let go of your desire to punish your partner and control the situation. The challenge for concerned people is to learn to express their emotions without letting their anxiety take over. This typically requires a certain degree of trust, which concerned people sometimes struggle with. The advice in the second part of this book is designed to help people work through these issues.

Concerned Partner *Betrays* Confident Partner	Confident Partner *Betrayed by* Concerned Partner
Motivation for Betrayal	**Reaction to Betrayal**
The Paradox of Intimacy and not feeling loved and appreciated creates the desire for attention and a need to assert oneself. "I don't think you care about me. So I sometimes impulsively do things I shouldn't because it makes me feel better in the moment."	Feeling disappointed, hurt, and confused. Being betrayed by a partner who says they are totally in love (a concerned individual) can be disorienting. "If you love me so much, why did you act that way?"

Concerned Partner *Betrays* Confident Partner

When concerned people love their partners and want to please them, but don't feel loved as much in return, they may start to disregard their partner's expectations and wind up betraying them. For example, part of what motivated Ashley (concerned) to cheat on Brian (confident) were her insecurities about their relationship—she doubted that he really loved her. So when Alex, an attractive guy from her gym, showed her the attention she wanted, she liked it. She had no intention of betraying Brian—that was the last thing she ever wanted to do—but she was just excited to talk to someone as attractive as Alex. At first, they just flirted, but after a while they started going to lunch together occasionally. Eventually, this increasing involvement led to a sexual encounter.

When an intimate betrayal comes to light, concerned people, like Ashley, typically feel so ashamed they're likely to deny that anything happened, act defensively, or profusely apologize and make promises to never do it again. Concerned individuals rush to fix problems because of their underlying anxiety, which makes it difficult for them to see past their own emotions and understand what their partners are going through.

Ashley didn't acknowledge Brian's feelings or the harm she'd done to their relationship. She was so consumed with her own discomfort—her fear of losing him (the very fear that caused this problem in the first place)— she couldn't acknowledge his perspective or give him what he needed in the moment. Brian, like most people, needed to have his feelings acknowledged.

If you have a concerned style of attachment and have betrayed your partner, it may be difficult to listen to the harm that you've caused your partner. To have any chance of reconciliation, you will have to learn how to take your time and make your partner feel understood without rushing to apologize and attempting to fix the problem.

Confident Partner *Betrayed by* Concerned Partner

Concerned partners work extra hard to please their partners, so when a betrayal comes to light, it doesn't make a lot of sense from the perspective of the confident individual.

Brian had little doubt that Ashley was in love with him. She was always going out of her way to make him feel special—she'd make his favorite dish when he had a rough day at work, try her best to get along with his sister, and listen to him whenever he was feeling down. To discover that she cheated on him blew his mind. He couldn't understand how someone who loved him so much could betray his trust in such a painful way. He had a very difficult time understanding why Ashley didn't tell him that she needed more attention. He struggled to see how she didn't want to burden him with her needs and instead reached out to someone else.

If you have a confident style of attachment and have been betrayed by a partner who has a concerned style of attachment, it helps to avoid blowing up at your partner. When concerned individuals are fearful, they have a difficult time listening to and empathizing with their partners. While concerned people often want to do what's best for their relationship, their anxiety can sometimes trip them up. If you can express your disappointment to your concerned partner in a way that is less likely to trigger their fear of abandonment, you will have an easier time talking about what happened and working with your partner to solve the problem.

Cool-Confident Pairings

Cool Partner *Betrays* Confident Partner

In general, people with cool styles of attachment are more likely than others to act against their partner's wishes and desires. Cool individuals experience relationships as overly constraining and struggle with intimacy in their relationships—they stress autonomy over interdependence.

Cool Partner *Betrays* Confident Partner	Confident Partner *Betrayed by* Cool Partner
Motivation for Betrayal	**Reaction to Betrayal**
The Paradox of Intimacy and strong need to be independent.	Feeling annoyed, disappointed, and resentful, but not completely surprised. Partner has always tried to avoid intimacy and closeness—the latest betrayal probably fits a pattern of one's partner putting himself or herself ahead of the relationship.
"Relationships are tough for me. I cannot lose sight of myself in this relationship. I often need to put my own needs first."	"Just another instance of you putting your needs ahead of mine."

While both concerned and confident people are comfortable giving up some of their freedom to be with their partners, cool people focus more of their attention on how their relationships make them feel trapped. Because they have a difficult time understanding their own emotions and perspectives, as well as their partner's, they often act with their own self-interest in mind. They also violate their partner's expectations because it helps them avoid feeling close to them ("I can do what I want!"). It's worth repeating: cool individuals often don't fully understand the emotions underlying their actions, and they don't like to reflect on their feelings and behavior—they try to avoid thinking about issues involving intimacy.

George is a classic example of someone with a cool style of attachment. Rather than consider Maria's feelings, he deals with his fears of intimacy by creating quasi-intimate scenarios with multiple people. In fact, he isn't being truly intimate or truthful with anyone, but by keeping a lot of people in the dark, George feels safe— no one is allowed to get too close to him.

When betrayals come to light, cool people don't like talking about it. They're quick to dismiss their partner's concerns as trivial and dislike talking about issues that involve expectations, intimacy, and trust, much less betrayal. Because discussing relational problems involves being open and making oneself vulnerable—behaviors that cool individuals try really hard to avoid—they tend to shut down when problems emerge. If they do react, they may lash out and try to blame their partner for their actions ("Look what you made me do") or quickly try to put the incident behind them ("It's over…let's move on"). Both tactics are just another way to create distance in their relationship. Rather than talk about what happened, they often just want to "put it in the past"—whatever that means.

If you're a cool individual and you've betrayed your partner's trust, you will have to get out of your comfort zone and explore the feelings that motivated your behavior. You will need to reflect on the emotions underlying your actions. Your partner will not be able to forgive you unless you provide a genuine explanation for your behavior.

Confident Partner *Betrayed by* Cool Partner

When Maria first found out that George had been having an affair, her first reaction was to freak out. After a few days of yelling at her husband, Maria realized that if she had any chance of saving her marriage, she needed to talk to him about what happened. Maria eventually asked her husband why he cheated on her.

Unfortunately, George didn't have an answer; he didn't understand why he cheated. He told her, "I don't know. I just messed up. Can you forgive me?" This is not what Maria wanted to hear. She needed to know *why* her husband betrayed her. Without understanding why he cheated in the first place, how could they even try to solve the problem? Maria was extremely frustrated with her husband's inability to explain his actions.

If you're a confident person, you know how difficult it can be to get through to a cool partner when dealing with any problem. Getting a cool person to understand your perspective and empathize with you can be quite challenging. In the chapters to come, we will provide advice for dealing with these issues.

Confident Partner *Betrays* Cool Partner Motivation for Betrayal	Cool Partner *Betrayed by* Confident Partner Reaction to Betrayal
The Paradox of Intimacy and their cool partner's neglectful attitude motivate them to put their own needs ahead of the relationship.	Angry and upset, but suspected that no one can be trusted—even kind and caring people will betray a partner's trust.
"Sometimes my partner is so distant and checked out that I just do what I want from time to time."	"I thought you were one of the good ones...guess I should've known better."

Confident Partner *Betrays* Cool Partner

Confident individuals are sometimes motivated to betray their cool partner because they find themselves in no-win situations. Their partners aren't terribly interested in what they're doing, and this indifference hurts. Although they don't want to betray their partner's trust, they're irritated that their partners don't seem to give a damn, so they sometimes push boundaries out of frustration.

For example, **Tyler** (confident) and **Jessica** (cool) have been dating for about a year and are starting to encounter some problems related to their attachment styles. Lately, Jessica seems checked out. She doesn't seem as interested in Tyler as she was when they started dating. She doesn't ask him questions about what's going on with him, and when he does try to share things with her, Jessica seems to be somewhere else. Tyler began to feel lonely in his relationship. Rather than discuss his feelings with her, he downloaded Tinder and started flirting with women. Tyler didn't want to meet someone else; he just wanted to feel as if someone was interested in him.

If you're a confident individual and your partner doesn't show a lot of interest in your relationship, it can be easy to put your own needs ahead of the relationship. While this is a common response to feeling neglected, there are better ways to deal with your feelings rather than betraying your partner's trust.

Cool Partner *Betrayed by* Confident Partner

Cool individuals are likely to downplay the importance of their relationships and aren't very motivated to try to work things out. It's also difficult for them to work at rebuilding trust because, in the process, they'll have to lower their guard to identify their expectations, explore their feelings, and disclose their insights with their partners. Easier said than done!

For example, when Jessica discovered Tyler had been chatting with women on Tinder, she'd had it. Jessica knew deep down not to trust others, so why should Tyler be any different? In the back of her mind, she knew he'd probably screw up their relationship somehow—maybe this was all she needed to know. At first Jessica was extremely upset, and then she just felt numb. She didn't want to deal with her feelings and talk about how Tyler violated her trust. She just decided to call it quits.

If you're a cool individual and have been betrayed by a confident partner, you're probably tempted to dismiss your relationship. However, this may be the ideal opportunity to learn new ways of dealing with problems in a relationship because confident people have the insights and skills needed to work through an intimate betrayal. Although you might be thinking about ending your relationship, consider this: if you get involved again, which you probably will, you'll almost certainly be betrayed again. Better to address the problem when it's the easiest to solve—when you're involved with a confident partner.

If you use this opportunity to learn how to express your feelings, talk about your expectations, and discuss issues as they arise, you'll probably be pleasantly surprised at the rewards. If you learn to manage closeness with another person, it can put you on the path to better physical health, mental acuity, and emotional stability.

Cool–Concerned Pairings

Cool Partner *Betrays* Concerned Partner **Motivation for Betrayal**	**Concerned Partner *Betrayed by* Cool Partner** **Reaction to Betrayal**
The Paradox of Intimacy and a strong motivation to assert independence because they consider their concerned partners overly needy and clingy (suffocating). "No one controls what I do. The more you try to control me, the more I will do as I please."	Feels totally out of control, scared, and resentful. Extremely angry and fearful because of their cool partner's blatant disregard for their concerns. Tries to control their partner in a futile attempt to feel safe. "How could you do this to me? You can't treat me like this! I won't let you! (But, I do)."

Concerned Partner *Betrays* Cool Partner **Motivation for Betrayal**	**Cool Partner *Betrayed by* Concerned Partner** **Reaction to Betrayal**
The Paradox of Intimacy and feeling neglected by a cool partner leads to frustration and anger. Acts against their partner's expectations out of hurt feelings and spite. "You don't really love me. I'm not going to be the only person in this relationship who is treated with a lack of respect."	Livid that a controlling and needy partner would turn around and violate their trust. Wants out of relationship or threatens to leave. "You're always trying to control me. And *you* had the nerve to betray *me*? You're completely messing up my life. I've had enough of you!"

A person with a cool style of attachment involved with someone with a concerned style of attachment is the definition of a problematic relationship. One person runs while the other chases. Both parties often bring out the worst in each other. Concerned partners try to control their cool partners, while cool partners find new ways to push their concerned partners away. This combination often results in an ongoing spiral of misery. Both parties are pushing each other's buttons with little gained except hurt feelings, anger, and frustration.

This is exactly the situation that Zachary and Jacob are going through. Jacob constantly feels overwhelmed by Zachary's needs, so he rebels. Jacob ignores Zachary's texts, flirts with other guys, and even tried to find a job on the opposite coast.

Zachary is extremely hurt by his boyfriend's behavior. He loves his boyfriend and just wants to be loved in return. When Jacob betrays his trust, Zachary feels panicky and confused—like he's losing his boyfriend and his life is spinning out of control. In an attempt to feel safe, Zachary tries to control what his boyfriend does. Sometimes he yells, cries, or even gives him the silent treatment in an attempt to get attention.

Zachary often ends up betraying Jacob as well. Zachary installed spyware on Jacob's computer so he could monitor what his boyfriend was really doing. When Jacob found out, he flipped out. He couldn't believe that his boyfriend would invade his privacy—in his mind, this was a betrayal far worse than anything he had done to Zachary.

By the way cool and concerned individuals interact with each other, they reinforce their attachment beliefs. Cool people, like Jacob, experience their partners as being overly needy and anxious. Concerned people, like

Zachary, watch as their partners try to create distance in their relationships. Both parties are experiencing their worst nightmares come true. Their partners are acting exactly as they fear. Such reactions bring out the unhealthiest aspects of intimacy—negativity, hostility, and fear.

Most couples don't fully realize the damage that such negative behavior inflicts on their relationship and each other. Research consistently shows that for any couple to truly be happy, negative reactions need to be kept in check. Couples need to be able to deal with their emotions, understand each other, and work as a team. When cool and concerned people couple up, they're more likely to do the opposite—they often let their emotions get out of hand, push each other's buttons, fight for their own perspectives, and turn their relationship into a battle of "you versus me." No one wins *that* fight.

If this situation is so toxic, what keeps cool and concerned people together? Other factors (such as physical attraction, cultural beliefs, family ties, and money) can play a role. Also, attachments—even toxic ones—are difficult to break. And cool and concerned individuals stay together for several other reasons. *People tend to accept the love they think they deserve.* For example, confident people expect to be treated with respect. When a confident person is consistently treated like crap, he or she is likely to leave. On the other hand, when one expects a partner to mistreat them, it should come as little surprise when they end up staying with a partner who does just that.

Put another way, cool and concerned people are likely to stay together, in part, because they think that's how love works. This is especially true when a cool man and a concerned woman get together because their attachment styles align with stereotypes about gender roles and behavior. When a cool man dates a concerned woman, they're likely to stay together despite the emotional costs because cool men think most women are anxious, and most concerned women think men are cool and distant.

In reality, there are all types of men and women. There are plenty of concerned men and cool women just as there are lots of men and women with a confident style of attachment. It's unfortunate that stereotypes about how relationships are supposed to work sometimes keep people in a troubled relationship.

Missing Matches

You'll notice that we've left out some of the possible combinations in our previous descriptions. Two people with certain matching attachment styles are less likely to form a relationship than others, but if they do, the relationship is likely to quickly fall apart.

Cool and Cool Pairings. When it comes to love and intimacy, at least one party has to do some of the heavy lifting. Someone has to engage in self-disclosure, make plans, call a partner back, and so on. Imagine two cool individuals trying to date; neither party is likely to make the effort to reach out to the other. It goes something like this: "You call me." "No, you call me." And no one calls. These types of relationships are fairly rare.

Concerned and Concerned Pairings. In this case, both parties are so concerned about their own emotions not being met that they lose sight of their partner's needs. It can come down to an emotional game of "You don't love me..." "No,

you don't love *me*." Concerned people are looking for a
stronger and wiser partner. Being emotionally involved
with a confident or cool person makes more sense than
being in a relationship with someone who feels just as
anxious about being loved. However, if they do become involved, some concerned-concerned pairings are likely to
engage in yo-yo dating—that is, a constant cycle of breaking up and getting back together. To the people involved
in such a relationship, it probably feels something like this:
"You don't love me. And you're too needy. I can't deal with
this. Let's break up. I feel so alone. Let's try again." And the
pattern repeats itself over and over.

We can see why some pairings are not likely to even
get started, or if they do, fall apart quickly. It's a case of
having a little too much in common.

Why Do People Stay with
the Wrong Partners?

Let's think about why people stay in any relationship,
good or bad. As we mentioned, the need for attachment
is the glue that helps keep couples together. The decision to stay together is also influenced by a wide range of
factors including various traits, qualities, or circumstances, including finances, physical appearance, intelligence,
personality, or shared cultural beliefs, among others.

Additionally, it helps to think about attachment styles
as a spectrum rather than a static trait. For instance,
some people are at the extreme end of having a confident style of attachment, while others are less confident.
As mentioned in Chapter 3, some people have a mixed or
blended style of attachment; they may have a confident

attachment style with either some cool or concerned tendencies mixed in. A confident person may stay with someone who's obnoxious because that confident person has some concerned characteristics as well.

Finally, it's useful to keep in mind that people do not consciously form attachments. Attachments are different from love and companionship. Attachments are the bonds that keep people together, whether the relationship involves happiness or heartache.

What Does This Mean for Your Relationship?

If you and your partner are in a toxic relationship—let's say, a cool and concerned pairing—the issues you're dealing with are probably larger than the betrayal you've uncovered. The advice provided in the second half of this book will be more effective if you—or you and your partner—work with a therapist. It took a long time for you to get into this situation, and it will take a long time for you to work your way out of it. The problems you face are not insurmountable; it will just take more effort and additional guidance to help you create a healthy, happy relationship with your current or future partner.

Putting It All Together

Discovering an intimate betrayal often leads people to seek out answers to questions they have about themselves, their partners, and their relationships. Having insight into your and your partner's style of attachment may not always be pleasant, but it will make it much easier to understand how you and your partner interact and therefore give you the tools you need to help solve the problems you're facing.

Takeaways

- Both your and your partner's style of interaction influence how betrayals are experienced.
- Two confident individuals have an easier time than others when working through a relational transgression.
- Broken trust, hurt feelings, anger, and resentment are common when cool and concerned people are in a relationship with each other.

CHAPTER 5

Common Pitfalls and Counterproductive Behaviors

WHEN FEELING *BETRAYED* or hurt, it's natural to want to blame your partner for what happened. And your partner may, in fact, be to blame. However, it's usually not so simple, because many, if not most, betrayals are due to relational dynamics—the actions of both parties over time. Just as it takes two people to create a positive outcome, it often takes two people to create problems. As the old saying goes, it takes two to tango, or in this case, tangle.

We know that this can be hard to hear, especially if you've been betrayed. However, specific pitfalls and counterproductive behaviors underlie many intimate transgressions. Being betrayed by a loved one is usually not an isolated incident, but is often tied to behaviors such as holding unrealistic expectations, using controlling language, and expressing disappointment through the use of hostility.

The good news is that reflecting on how your actions may have unknowingly contributed to the problems in your relationship can be empowering. Such insight can help you change your behavior and break out of endless cycles of arguments, broken promises, and betrayals. When reflecting on your behavior, it also helps to view the situation from the perspective of an objective outsider: how would a neutral party evaluate both your and your partner's behavior?

Assessing Your Expectations

There is a direct link between the expectations you hold and how a partner will betray your trust. According to the Paradox of Intimacy, we place the most expectations on the people we are closest to. You probably don't place a ton of expectations on a stranger, but when you become romantically involved with someone, you start to care about almost everything that person does—from minor issues concerning their appearance to larger issues such as the values they express.

When reflecting on *how* the expectations you place on your romantic partner may have contributed to the betrayal, it helps to think of expectations along a spectrum. Some people place few expectations on their romantic partners. For the most part, these people don't care what their partners do; they have given up and let their partners do whatever they please. This often happens when individuals feel trapped in a relationship, and for whatever reason, they are unable (or unwilling) to call it quits—a low-reward, low-maintenance relationship.

Other people place moderate expectations on their partners. People who hold moderate expectations inhabit the middle ground; while they don't give up on their romantic relationships, they don't idealize them. They tend not to believe in romantic, passionate love or that their partners should be flawless. Instead, they take a more practical approach, settling for a relationship based on comfort and convenience. They don't expect their partners to mistreat them, but they also don't expect their partners to go out of their way to make them feel special. These couples have settled into a comfortable routine, which lacks many of the benefits of intimacy while minimizing the risks of being betrayed.

Major betrayals, however, are more common when people place unrealistic expectations on their romantic partners. Unrealistic expectations are standards that are extremely difficult to live up to. Most unrealistic expectations involve issues related to closeness and intimacy—like the idea that a partner should always understand your perspective or shouldn't have sexual feelings for someone else.

Unrealistic expectations stem from both the act of falling in love as well as cultural notions about love and romance. Love is a very powerful emotion. When we're in love, it's inevitable that we want to believe the best about our partners and relationships, even if those beliefs aren't practical or based in reality. Our culture and society also promote the idea that true love involves finding your soul mate—someone who will always understand you and act with your best interest at heart—the Hollywood version of romantic love where couples find their perfect match and live happily ever after.

Holding unrealistic expectations is problematic because partners often feel inadequate when they fail to live up to such high standards. They may question if the relationship is right for them and may become reluctant to share their feelings. If your partner doesn't always agree with you, or your sex life isn't always mind-blowing, or your partner develops a small crush on someone else, your partner may start to feel as if something is going wrong, whether it is or not. Keep in mind that these types of experiences are normal; it's common for people to have contradictory feelings and doubts about their relationships. But if you hold unrealistic relational beliefs, these experiences can take on an overly negative meaning for both you and your partner: "If we were truly in love, this wouldn't be happening."

Almost always, feeling inadequate or falling short of what's expected can lead to some form of concealment and a lack of genuine sharing. Ironically, it's expecting too much from a partner that creates exactly the opposite of what people really want: a caring, supportive relationship.

How can you tell if your expectations are unrealistic? Consider the expectations you place on your partner. Could *you* live up to the expectations you place on him or her? Do you think that most people could? If not, your expectations are probably going to clash with reality at some point or another.

It also helps to be down-to-earth about what love and romance entail. While the fun part of love tricks us into

Realistic View of Love

Even in the healthiest relationships people will...

- need some space.
- have disagreements on substantive issues.
- have feelings—even sexual ones—for someone else.
- occasionally put their own needs ahead of what's best for the relationship.

thinking our partners are perfect, realistic love involves working with an imperfect partner when he or she disappoints you. True love entails working through the inevitable and difficult aspects of intimacy in a thoughtful, caring, and respectful way. Love requires understanding a partner's perspective when you've been hurt, trying to find common ground when the situation looks bleak, and going the extra mile to try to rebuild trust.

When you discover a major betrayal, there are several issues to consider regarding your expectations. Are they realistic? And have you communicated them effectively?

If you're holding unrealistic expectations, you're placing both you and your partner in a no-win situation. Your partner can't possibly meet your expectations, and you will be hurt, disappointed, and betrayed. To help you identify your expectations, picture your ideal partner, whether it's your current one or a fantasy partner. Write down all of the qualities and characteristics you'd like your ideal partner to possess (examples might be nice, honest, and/or faithful) as well as the specific ways you would like to be treated (such as talk to me about issues before they become problems, be involved with my family and friends, or spend Saturdays with me).

Now arrange your expectations from most important to least important. Now look at the items on the top of your list. Are these expectations realistic? Do you think the average person could meet these expectations? Even if your partner is exceptional, at some time or another, their behavior is likely to fall close to how most people behave. Again, it helps to keep in mind that even decent, considerate people are *still* human.

We aren't saying that you shouldn't hold high expectations about your romantic partner. In fact, for a relationship to be successful, it's important to have very high, but realistic expectations.

So what's the difference between high versus unrealistic expectations? Unrealistic expectations have no chance of being met, while high expectations are demanding but doable. For example, it's not realistic to expect your romantic partner to never develop feelings for another person. It's realistic, however, to expect your romantic partner not to act on such feelings.

Setting high expectations is one of the most effective ways to bring out the best in a romantic partner and your relationship. Setting high expectations is important because it keeps a relationship interesting, creates intimacy, and results in more rewarding outcomes. Being pushed to improve your life is, in fact, stimulating. Challenging your partner to meet your expectations helps keep his or her focus on your relationship.

After Brian realized that Ashley strayed because she wasn't getting the attention she needed, he looked for ways to become more involved in her life. For example, Brian decided to push Ashley to get in better shape and help her get a promotion at work. So he started daring her to go for short runs with him after work and longer ones on the weekend. He also began to encourage her to talk about the obstacles she is facing in her job, and he carefully listened to her ideas for dealing with them. Sometimes Brian even encouraged Ashley to role-play difficult vendor-client disputes with him.

Ashley appreciates all of Brian's efforts because he's helping her improve her life in ways that matter to her. Given that most people like to be challenged in certain aspects of their lives, shouldn't *you* be the one to push your partner to do so? If you're not challenging your partner and creating intimacy, there's a possibility that someone else will.

Communicating Your Expectations

It should go without saying that both you and your partner should be comfortable sharing your expectations with each other. It's impossible to build a relationship when your expectations are not clear. You and your partner don't have to agree on everything, but couples who know what's expected of each other have a better chance of making their relationships work. It's important to discuss what issues you agree on and what differences exist. Having such truthful exchanges creates more intimacy, trust, and respect—and decreases the risk of disappointment and broken trust.

Research shows that having explicit discussions about your relational expectations can help you avoid many of the problems that couples encounter such as misunderstandings, hurt feelings, and confusion. Research also shows that the simple task of sharing expectations is anything but simple.

In some cases, people don't take the time to reflect on their expectations or communicate them with their partners. Some couples "slide" into commitments without ever discussing what they expect from each other. Picture the couple who moves in together because they're already spending so much time together and think it would be a great way to save money, but they don't discuss what moving in together means. Perhaps one person sees moving in together as nothing more than a temporary financial windfall, while the other person sees it as

Expectations about Living Together

Couples do better when they make their expectations explicit.
Such a discussion could involve any or all of the following:

- I want to grow closer to you.
- I expect to have sex a lot more often.
- I need some time to myself in the mornings and right
  after work, for example.
- I don't want you to play your music when I'm home.
- I don't want the TV blasting in the living room while I'm
  trying to work.
- I expect you to be on your best behavior around my
  friends, family, and coworkers.
- I expect you to respect my privacy—don't go through my
  personal things, journal, mail/email, or text messages.
- I expect you to do small things for me at least once a
  week—like buying me flowers, watching a movie I like, or
  giving me a back rub.
- I expect you to work out with me every morning.

a stepping-stone toward a more permanent emotional
commitment. When couples don't talk about their expectations, trouble is sure to follow.

Even when couples talk about their expectations, that
doesn't necessarily mean that they understand each other. When sharing expectations, it's important for couples
to communicate their goals and wishes using simple and
unambiguous language. For example, if one of your expectations is to grow closer to your partner, what exactly
does that mean? Does it mean that you want to merge
your finances? Have more heartfelt conversations? Have
more passionate sex? Or when someone says, "I'd like

us to spend more time together," what does that really mean? Sitting together in front of the TV? Or spending more time talking about what's going on in each other's lives? Or even when someone says, "I need you to help out more around the house," does that mean taking out the trash, cleaning the whole house, or something very specific like cleaning the toilet?

Using descriptive rather than abstract language can help you avoid many problems and pitfalls when trying to make your expectations clear. Descriptive language spells out the details of what you have in mind, while abstract language is vague. For example, telling your partner you would like them to "come home by 10 P.M." defines your expectations clearly. Asking a partner to "come home early" is obscure and can be interpreted in different ways.

Similarly, when couples start "dating," what does that mean? Are they seeing each other exclusively? Or are they going on dates and seeing other people as well? *Dating* is an ambiguous word; it means different things to different people. For instance, when Zachary and Jacob started dating, Jacob continued to chat with other guys. For him, dating didn't mean that he was only going to see Zachary. Of course, Zachary didn't see it that way.

It's also important to *confirm* that your partner clearly understands what's expected. When discussing important expectations, ask your partner to paraphrase the discussion (you might say, "Just to be clear, what did we agree to?"). Expressing expectations and making sure you've been understood is critical because it takes the guesswork out of knowing what's expected. It helps avoid the conflicts, fights, and betrayals many couples experience and is essential in building a genuine, intimate relationship.

Expectations and Attachment Styles

The kinds of expectations we hold for our partners and relation-ships are also influenced by our attachment style. *Confident* individuals are more likely than others to set high but realistic expectations about a romantic partner, and they also communi-cate their expectations more effectively. *Concerned* people, on the other hand, are much more likely to hold unrealistic expec-tations about their romantic partners, which often leads to frus-tration and disappointment. Such negative feelings often lead to the use of more controlling language and displays of hostility, thus creating the type of environment where intimate betrayals are more likely to occur. Finally, individuals with a *cool* style of attachment are the least likely to place a lot of demands on their romantic partners, but they're also the least likely to reap the benefits that intimacy creates.

Holding high expectations is tricky; it requires identi-fying a core set of expectations and learning how to com-municate them effectively, while also keeping in mind that there's no such thing as a trouble-free relationship.

Counterproductive Behavior and Intimate Betrayals

Again, being betrayed by an intimate partner is usually not a random event. Broken promises and transgressions can be easily predicted once you learn to recognize the contributing factors. Many of the factors underlying a re-lational betrayal boil down to how effectively couples com-municate with each other. In every relationship, couples not only set expectations, but they also struggle with issues of power and control, engage in conflict, express disappointment, and so on. How couples talk about these issues directly affects when and how the truth is told.

For example, consider **Ethan** and **Hannah** who have been married for five years and have been struggling with a pattern of recurring betrayals related to their finances. They have very different attitudes about spending money. Ethan has a carefree attitude and is overly generous. He frequently invites people out for dinner and lends his friends money. Hannah likes to spend money, too, but on family vacations and romantic getaways.

One evening, a friend invited them to a birthday party at a nearby restaurant. Ethan bought the first round of drinks, but when he was getting ready to order another round, Hannah became annoyed. While she was happy to go to the party with him, she didn't want him to pay for everyone's bar tab. When she told him that he needed to let someone else get the next round, Ethan felt embarrassed and disrespected; he didn't like being told what to do, especially in front of their friends. So rather than respect her request, he went ahead and bought the next round.

Hannah had had enough. The two of them had been down this road before, but this time she became angry and stormed out of the party. Ethan, not wanting to ruin the evening, pretended that everything was fine. When the check for dinner came, he insisted on paying for it. When he got home, a huge fight erupted. Both parties felt disrespected and misunderstood and took their frustrations out on each other. To make matters worse, Ethan neglected to tell her about paying for everyone's dinner. When the truth eventually came out, Hannah exploded.

Ethan and Hannah blamed each other for the fight, but in reality, they both played a role in the night's events.

Controlling Language. Controlling language involves talking in a way that makes the other person feel as if he or she has no say in the matter. It can range from telling a partner what he or she can do all the way to making threats and ultimatums. While controlling language is clear-cut, it's not a great way to get someone to do what you want. It can, in fact, be counterproductive because it leads to resistance. None of us like to have our choices or free will taken from us. Controlling language makes people feel constrained, disregarded, and disrespected—it highlights the constraints of being in a relationship. People who are on the receiving end of controlling language are likely to rebel and fight back in an attempt to reassert themselves and gain a sense of control.

This is what happened with Hannah and Ethan. Because Hannah frequently tells Ethan exactly how he can spend money, he often feels belittled. He then deals with his feelings by doing the opposite of what Hannah wants, and she ends up feeling betrayed. Relationships work best when they're based on open discussions and mutual decision-making. Sharing a life requires openness, flexibility, and creating something new. Using controlling language goes against a genuine partnership.

It's just as important to discuss your expectations in a nonthreatening manner. We often hear couples discuss their expectations using threats and ultimatums—for instance, making statements such as, "If you ever…I'll break both your legs." While making such statements definitely gets the point across, doing so is far from ideal if you want your partner to tell you the truth. Remember, lying to a partner is driven by fear—fear of hurting a partner or getting in trouble. If you threaten or imply punishing your partner for not living up to your expectations, you can be sure of the following: your partner will hide mistakes from you.

If you use *controlling language,* you're more likely to increase your chances of being deceived by the person you love.

Expressing Hostility. We all get pissed off at our partners on occasion. It's *how* you express your feelings that matters the most. If you express your negative feelings by showing hostility, raising your voice, yelling, screaming, making a scene, attacking your partner, or giving the silent treatment, it's probably doing more harm than good.

Expressing negative feelings in a punishing manner creates a climate of fear. We instinctively respond to fear by taking steps to protect ourselves, and the most common way is to shut down and hide what's going on. Simply put, if you react poorly when your partner tells you the truth—that is, you punish them for something they have said or done—your partner will quickly learn that it's not safe to be open and honest with you.

A trivial, but common example illustrates the problem of using hostility to get your point across. **Lou** and **Mary** have been married for more than thirty years. During Lou's last medical exam, his cholesterol level turned out to be dangerously high; he had to make dramatic changes in his diet and start a serious exercise routine. When he occasionally slips up and has a bacon cheeseburger with fries—his favorite meal—Mary freaks out. Her anger comes out, and she lets him have it: "Are you trying to kill yourself?!"

Mary's negative emotions arise from her desire to achieve her goal—to get Lou to change his behavior so he can be healthy. But, instead, they've had the opposite effect—Lou has learned that if he eats a cheeseburger, he needs to do it behind her back.

We're not saying that you shouldn't express your disapproval or other negative feelings. In fact, it's critical to express how you're feeling if you want to have any type of genuine relationship. You just need to be careful *how* you express those feelings. If Mary expressed her frustration in a way that didn't make Lou feel judged, he might have decided to give up his fatty meals. Rather than getting upset, she could have told her husband why the behavior was important to her: "I'm afraid of losing you and don't want that to happen. When I see you eat a cheeseburger, I worry."

An honest, open relationship can't thrive if you express your negative feelings in a way that creates fear and encourages deception. Genuine, honest conversations—the kind needed to create closeness and intimacy—can't happen when people feel intimidated.

Moving Forward

If you're unsure if you use controlling language and express disappointment in negative, hostile ways, you might want to ask people who know you well for their perspective. Ask them, "Do I come across as being controlling? Do you think I handle disappointment well?" Getting your partner's take on this can be very revealing. We don't always see ourselves the way that other people do.

What do you do if you realize that you come across as somewhat controlling or have the tendency to let your negative emotions get the best of you? To begin with, don't beat yourself up. Engaging in self-blame isn't wise or helpful; it doesn't help people solve problems. The best thing to do is to focus on the big picture. Focus on what you hope to achieve. What are your goals? Do you want to try to solve the problem? Create more intimacy and closeness? Rebuild trust?

In addition to focusing on your goals, try to adopt a more analytical approach to your behavior. Rather than view your behavior as a problem, focus on your actions going forward in terms of their *effectiveness*. Look at your behavior from the role of an outsider. Do your actions help you accomplish your goal? If you're trying to create trust and intimacy, does yelling at your partner help you achieve the desired outcome? If not, that behavior wasn't effective.

Focusing on your goals and assessing your behavior in terms of its effectiveness can help you find a pathway forward and prevent you from falling into the trap of engaging in self-blame. It's easier to change your behavior when you think about your actions in terms of what works, rather than thinking about yourself in terms of right or wrong, good or bad. Throughout the rest of this book, we will provide specific advice for communicating with your partner in the most effective way possible when trying to recover from a major betrayal.

Putting It All Together

Intimate betrayals are often best understood by looking at what both partners bring to their relationship. While it's natural to want to blame your partner for betraying your trust, it's also useful to examine how your actions may have played a role—by reflecting on how you and your partner ended up in the situation. To prevent relational transgressions from happening—or happening again—you not only have to find ways to change your partner's behaviors, you may also need to learn how to change a few of your own. Acknowledging the idea that your behavior may have influenced, even in a small way, an intimate betrayal can be empowering. Increased awareness of how you may have unknowingly influenced events gives you power to change future outcomes.

Takeaways

- Holding unrealistic expectations sets relationships up for failure.
- High, realistic expectations can set the foundation for creating a meaningful and rewarding relationship.
- Using controlling language and expressing negativity in a hostile way can increase the risk of being betrayed by a partner.
- The best way to change your behavior going forward is to evaluate the way you communicate with your partner in terms of its effectiveness.

PART II

Solutions for Rebuilding Trust and Creating a Healthy Relationship

CHAPTER 6

Honoring Your Emotions

U NCOVERING AN INTIMATE betrayal can create intense feelings of panic, anger, fear, shock, sadness, and disappointment. Being betrayed by a romantic partner can also trigger feelings of loss and uncertainty— uncertainty about your partner, your relationship, and yourself. All of these emotions vary greatly depending on the individuals involved as well as the circumstances.

In fact, discovering a betrayal is often a more painful experience than being rejected outright. When you've been rejected, you have little choice but to move on. But when you've been betrayed, you're still involved with someone who has devalued you and your relationship, and it can hurt like hell! In fact, the emotional pain can feel like physical pain—as if you've been punched in the gut. We're wired to react strongly when we've been disrespected and devalued.

Because betrayals trigger intense emotions and they are typically discovered by accident, most people are not prepared to deal with the emotional aftermath. For example, you might walk in on your partner and catch him or her in the act (whatever the "act" may be). Perhaps you heard a voice-mail message not meant for you, or someone said they saw your partner in an out-of-town restaurant when he was supposed to be at the office. Yes, most unpleasant truths are stumbled upon, not sought out.

For instance, while Hannah was aware that she and Ethan had issues related to their finances, she assumed that everything else in their relationship was OK. That was until one morning she couldn't find her phone while Ethan was out on a run. She had promised to call her mom, so she grabbed Ethan's phone instead. Hannah was shocked when she discovered sexually explicit text messages between Ethan and one of his female coworkers, Stephanie.

The wave of emotions Hannah experienced was intense. She was shocked, hurt, and angry. When Ethan got back from his run, she let him have it. Hannah demanded to know what was going on and accused Ethan of being unfaithful. At first Ethan denied everything. He said the messages between Stephanie and him were just playful banter—an inside joke between two colleagues.

Of course that explanation didn't sit well with Hannah, so she continued to press him for an explanation. Eventually, Ethan responded to Hannah by matching her anger with hostility. He screamed at her, telling her she was crazy, and a terrible fight ensued. Fighting back and forth, as well as the original betrayal itself, does real damage to a relationship. When couples engage in personal attacks, it tends to stomp out any feelings of intimacy, closeness, and trust.

While attacking a partner who has betrayed you in an attempt to end a relationship is definitely an appropriate response in certain circumstances, that's not always the case. Many people unnecessarily cast aside an otherwise healthy relationship because they don't know how to work through an intimate betrayal. Dealing with a betrayal is never easy, but if you learn how to manage and express your emotions with the advice provided here, you may not only discover how to resolve your relationship problems more quickly, but you may grow closer together as a couple. It may seem counterintuitive, but—unless it's a deal breaker—discovering a betrayal can make a relationship stronger, if dealt with effectively.

Don't Blame Yourself

For starters, feelings of uncertainty can sometimes lead to self-doubt and self-blame ("Why didn't I see this coming?" or "Is there something wrong with me?"). Don't blame yourself for what happened. Your partner is responsible for their actions. Whatever you may have done, your partner made a choice—no matter what your partner says, you did not "make" them betray you.

And it's natural to question why this happened to you. While betrayals are common, no one wants to think it could happen in their relationship. In fact, the closer you get to someone, the more you want to believe that your partner is both faithful and truthful. This "truth-bias"—the tendency to believe that someone you love wouldn't deceive you—is one of the most well-documented biases people hold.

Truth-bias is what allows our relationships to flourish because we can only have truly loving relationships when we're biased to think our partners are being honest and genuine. On the other hand, if you were constantly suspicious and assumed everyone was fundamentally dishonest, developing a romantic relationship would be very difficult, if not impossible.

It's a catch-22 situation: By trusting someone, you put yourself at risk. But if you don't trust anyone, you will end up alone. There's no getting around the Paradox of Intimacy, and one must accept the possibility of the bad in order to experience the good. For example, if Hannah hadn't trusted Ethan to be faithful, she wouldn't have married him in the first place.

So if you're blaming yourself for the betrayal that happened or for not seeing it coming, give yourself some credit; the fact that you were betrayed means you're a normal, loving, trusting human being.

Typical Ways People Respond

Adopting a constructive approach to managing your emotions is easier when you understand how you initially respond to being betrayed by a romantic partner. Increased self-awareness coupled with knowledge about how our emotions work can help you identify more constructive ways of coping with your feelings when dealing with a relational setback. There are three common ways that people respond to the discovery of a major betrayal. Try to identify which emotional reaction best describes your behavior, and see the cause and effect of such a response.

Explosive Reactions. Some people respond to the discovery of betrayal by attacking their partner in a hostile and accusatory manner. Such responses can include overt displays of hostility, name-calling, and other attempts to humiliate your partner. For example, when Zachary discovered that Jacob was looking for jobs on the West Coast, he freaked out. He yelled, screamed, and confronted Jacob saying, "You piece of shit. How could you do this to me? I'm trying to build a life with you, and you've been lying to me. What kind of person does that?"

Hostile and humiliating attacks are often accompanied by attempts to manipulate and control a partner's behavior. Sometimes people threaten to make a scene in public or on social media or even threaten to hurt themselves or their partner. They may also get others involved, such as friends, coworkers, and other family members, including their own children. For example, Hannah threatened to go to Ethan's workplace and confront Stephanie face-to-face. Explosive reactions are often used to force a partner to admit their guilt and immediately change their behavior.

Given that most betrayals are discovered by accident and trigger strong emotional responses, it should come as little surprise that explosive reactions are common. When caught off guard by threatening information, many people react in the moment without taking time to actually experience their feelings and think about how they would like to respond. And when people have been hurt, there is an instinctual desire to get even—to punish a partner. There is also a tendency to want to attack whoever else may have been involved—to lash out at the "other person." If a partner acts in ways that make you feel disrespected and devalued, it can be hard not to want your partner or someone else to pay a price for their actions.

Explosive reactions to discovering an intimate betrayal are also more common for people who strongly identify with their feelings. Certain individuals, mostly people with a concerned style of attachment, have a difficult time separating themselves from their emotional reactions. Everyone has emotional reactions. However, some individuals have a more difficult time realizing that they have an identity that is separate from the emotions they're currently experiencing. Some individuals believe that their emotional reactions are who they are, rather than viewing their feelings as a temporary reaction to the current situation (more on this to come).

When people overidentify with their emotions, they actually feel their emotions more intensely and are more likely to instantly act on them instead of using their emotions to reflect on the problem at hand. At an unconscious level, people who overidentify with their emotions are thinking, "If I quickly and strongly act out, my partner will respond the way I want, which will make these awful feelings go away." But this is *not* what happens. Explosive emotional reactions eventually lead to more problems in a relationship.

People who engage in explosive reactions may also bring up other issues outside of the specific betrayal. When Hannah confronted Ethan about sexting with a coworker, she also brought up a long list of grievances related to her feeling devalued. She accused Ethan of constantly working late, skipping out on plans with her family, and spending too much time with his friends.

While explosive reactions *may* work for short periods of time—you might be able to control your partner's actions for a while and gain some temporary emotional relief—in the long run, it will not help you or your relationship. When fear, not empathy, causes a partner to change their behavior, it's only a matter of time before you'll be betrayed again. The more a partner feels constrained, the more likely they are to act out (the Paradox of Intimacy). Not only are you more likely to be hurt again, but negative and humiliating outbursts can do real damage to a relationship.

Attacking a partner, even one who betrayed you, is counterproductive because it shifts attention to your partner as an individual instead of focusing attention on how their *actions* impacted you. Such hostile attacks produce feelings of shame and prevent partners from listening to what's being said. True and meaningful resolution of the issue can only occur if and when your partner empathizes with your situation. Attacking a partner shuts down any empathetic response and creates a defensive environment where getting at the truth and finding a potential solution, if one exists, is increasingly difficult to do. If you learn how to reflect on your emotions before you act on them, you'll more likely express your feelings in ways that create empathy, which will more likely motivate your partner to take responsibility for his or her actions, understand them, and take the steps necessary to change his or her behavior.

If this pattern of explosive behavior describes how you tend to act, it's important to learn how to work through your emotional reactions, by honoring your feelings before engaging your partner. Your emotions aren't telling you what to do; your emotions are a tool designed to alert you to issues that need to be carefully thought through.

Although it's not going to be easy to remain even tempered when you have the next conversation with your partner, the more you practice working with your emotions, the easier it gets. This is not to say that you shouldn't show any emotions or assert yourself. It's just helpful to fully understand your emotions and express yourself in ways that are more likely to help you achieve your goal: to make you feel understood and help resolve the problem at hand. If you've already had an explosive outburst over what happened, cut yourself some slack. No one is perfect. When you start using more constructive ways of working with and sharing your emotions, you'll see progress.

Dismissive Reactions. Unlike those who fly into explosive reactions, people with dismissive reactions try to block out their emotions. As a result, they don't experience a lot of emotional uncertainty and self-blame ("Why did this happen to me?"). In fact, because such individuals avoid experiencing their emotional reactions, they have a hard time even describing what they are feeling.

People who engage in dismissive reactions work hard at keeping their emotions under wraps, until their defenses drop and they snap—lashing out in intense bouts of anger ("You suck!"). In other words, they ignore feelings like a crack in a windshield until it finally breaks through and can't be ignored any more. This often results in a volatile, relationship-ending outburst. They blame their partners for what happened without trying to understand what went wrong or how to make things better.

After they expel their emotions, they are quick to shut back down, leaving themselves little motivation to try to work things out. The hostility, scorn, and anger they direct toward their partners is not an attempt to resolve the issues, but instead is an attempt to push the problem away so they don't have to deal with their feelings. Such reactions are also good at pushing partners away.

It should come as little surprise that individuals with a cool style of attachment, who fear intimacy and closeness, are more likely to react dismissively when problems in their relationships arise.

This type of emotional reaction is clearly counter-productive. Pushing partners away and sweeping issues under the rug don't solve problems. In fact, people who act this way are more likely to see their relationships fall apart only to get into another relationship where the exact same pattern repeats itself.

Consider **Marcus** and his girlfriend **Sarah** who moved in together after dating for two years. Shortly afterward, Marcus caught Sarah chatting online with another guy. Rather than discuss his feelings and talk about the situation with her, he yelled at her, "You're a @#$%&! Get out of my life!" and that was the end of it. This wasn't the first time he bailed on a relationship rather than address how the situation made him feel—nor will it be his last.

If this pattern of behavior describes how you react, learning how to deal with your emotions differently can open up new ways of solving problems and lead to better outcomes for yourself and your relationship. It's better to learn how to deal with these issues in the present, rather than getting involved in a never-ending series of troubled relationships.

Constructive Reactions. When confronted with a breach of trust and other relationship problems, some people have an easier time dealing with their emotional reactions. While they experience anger, disappointment, and doubt, they also tend to reflect on their emotions in a more productive way. People who have explosive reactions are prone to rumination, exaggeration, and personal attacks; and those who have dismissive reactions are likely to push their partners away and move on. By contrast, those who take a constructive approach are more likely to honor their emotions and express them in a way that gains their partner's empathy.

Let's use **Adam** and his wife **Nadine** to illustrate the differences among explosive, dismissive, and constructive reactions to an intimate betrayal. Adam and Nadine recently dealt with a problem that many married couples face: how to best spend their money. The specific issue involved how much to spend on a wedding gift for a friend. They decided on $150. Adam was shocked when he received a call from the bride. She wanted to personally thank Adam and Nadine for the Tiffany crystal vase she received; it was not on their registry, and she was overwhelmed by their thoughtfulness and generosity. Adam immediately looked up the charges for the vase online. His wife had spent more than a thousand dollars on the gift, and he was livid.

Let's see how the three types of reactions might play out.

Explosive Reaction

Implicit Goal: To punish and control a partner.

Examples: "I just found out how much you spent
                      on the wedding gift. You went be-
                      hind my back and spent more than
                      we agreed to. I'm so pissed right now.
                      You're going to have to make this
                      right somehow!"

"What were you thinking? You spent a thousand dollars on a wedding gift? Are you crazy? You know we don't have money to throw around like that! I'm never going to let you do anything like that again!"

Likely Outcomes: Defensiveness, unresolved conflict, more lies and deception.

Dismissive Reaction

Implicit Goal: To be done with the issue and push a partner away.

Examples: "I just found out how much you spent on the wedding gift! Unbelievable! Steer clear of me for a while!"

"You spent a thousand dollars on a wedding gift? What's the point in talking to you? You can't be trusted with anything!"

Likely Outcomes: Less intimacy and closeness and the problem never gets addressed.

Constructive Reaction

Implicit Goal: To gain a partner's empathy and co-operation.

Examples: "I need to bring something up. I
                       found out how much money was
                       spent on the wedding gift. I'm frus-
                       trated, and I want to talk about it."

                       "I just found out how much was spent
                       on the wedding gift. I'm hurt and
                       disappointed. Can we talk?"

Likely Outcomes: A partner who is willing to listen and
                   talk about the issue.

Constructive approaches are useful because they give people the opportunity to, first, express their feelings and, second, to notice how their partner responds. And a partner's response to a constructive attempt to discuss the betrayal can be very telling. Couples eventually have to have a constructive, cooperative conversation in order to resolve and possibly recover from a relational transgression. The sooner you can get your partner to see the situation from your perspective, the better.

If the constructive reaction describes how you handle problems, you most likely have a confident style of attachment; you're good at acknowledging your feelings and expressing your emotions to your partner in ways that move the conversation forward. You might blow up from time to time, but you quickly reflect on the situation, honor your emotions, and try to find productive ways to discuss the issue with your partner. Dealing with your emotions constructively, however, is only the first of many things couples have to do in order to reestablish trust.

How to Honor Your Emotions

Research shows that it can be very powerful to take a step back and reflect on how our emotions work. Your feelings are real and genuine, and no one, not even your partner, can take your emotional experiences away from you. It may help to keep this in mind, especially if your partner tries to discount what you're going through.

With that said, our emotions are just one aspect of who we are, and, as you're likely well aware, they can change from moment to moment. So while it's great to acknowledge and honor our feelings, it's not helpful to overidentify with them. Put another way, it helps to be aware of what you're feeling, but don't feel that you have to immediately *act* on your emotions. It's possible and tremendously helpful to learn how to experience and observe your emotions rather than instantly acting on them (in a moment, we will provide a technique for helping you do this).

It helps to recognize your emotions for what they are and what they are not. Think of your emotions as a monitor, alerting you to opportunities and problems that warrant your attention. Viewing emotions as a monitor explains why it's necessary to honor them. If you ignore a monitor, it's designed to send stronger and stronger signals in an attempt to get your attention. Honoring your emotions is like telling the monitor you got the message, which helps quiet it down. But while our emotions alert us to problems, they are not designed to solve them.

To better understand the role of emotions in our lives, we've borrowed an analogy developed by Dan Siegel, an interpersonal neurobiologist at UCLA, who studies attachment and interpersonal relationships. Imagine that your hand is your brain. Open your hand and turn your palm toward you. Now fold your thumb over the palm of your hand so it's pointing at your little finger. Your thumb represents your limbic system—the warm, emotional part of your brain—which monitors your life and alerts you to events, like a betrayal, that need your attention. While our thumbs alert us to trouble, they are not designed to solve complex problems.

Look at your hand again. Now gently fold your fingers over your thumb. Your fingers represent your frontal lobe, the part of your mind responsible for complex problem solving and thoughtful behavior. This is your cool, rational side. Greater awareness of how your emotional and rational systems work together to solve problems will give you greater control over your feelings and make it easier for you to engage your partner using constructive techniques and strategies.

Research shows that engaging in this simple activity, which reinforces how your mind is naturally designed to work, can help you honor your emotions in ways that let you solve problems more effectively. As an exercise, the next time you notice you're having an emotional reaction (regarding the betrayal or something else), place your thumb across your palm while saying to yourself, "My thumb is trying to alert me to a potential problem." Then gently place your fingers over your thumb while saying to yourself, "I got the message. I'll let my fingers handle it from here."

When we acknowledge our feelings and reflect on ways to respond, we are engaging both parts of our mind as they were designed to work. The more you practice working with your emotions this way, the more adept you will become at managing them.

Understanding What You're Feeling

When feeling overwhelmed with negative emotions, it's important to take the time to acknowledge and experience your feelings. This piece of advice may sound somewhat naive. Of course you're experiencing emotions—and intense ones at that! You were just betrayed! But part of the problem when dealing with a transgression is that people don't like to fully feel their emotions. No one likes to be in pain, so most people try to move from *hurting* to *blaming* as fast as they can. Blaming a partner or someone else involved often feels better than feeling hurt, scared, sad, or other emotions. But to truly resolve your problem, you must first understand your own feelings. Unless you fully understand what you're feeling, you'll have a more difficult time explaining your experience to your partner in a calm and constructive way, which is the only way you will gain their true cooperation.

Common Emotions People Feel When Betrayed

- Afraid
- Angry
- Apprehensive
- Confused
- Disappointed
- Disgusted
- Embarrassed
- Furious
- Heartbroken
- Helpless
- Hopeless
- Inadequate
- Insecure
- Livid
- Lost
- Nervous
- Sad
- Uncertain
- Vengeful
- Vulnerable

What core emotions are you experiencing? Sadness? Fear? Disappointment? All of them?

It helps to identify and describe the feelings brought about by the betrayal. That is, what *you're feeling* rather than what your partner *did*. This may be harder than you realize. Get a notebook and start describing your emotions. As we mentioned in the Introduction, you'll get more out of this book by completing each step before moving on to the next one. So go ahead and get started.

Again, don't write down what happened; rather, focus on your emotional reactions to what happened. For example, instead of writing down that your partner cheated on you, identify how you felt when you found out the truth. It could go something like this: "Right now, I'm feeling hurt, angry, sad, disappointed, confused, betrayed..." or whatever emotion comes to mind. Research shows that identifying emotions, even if only to yourself, helps you calm down and gain clarity when dealing with stressful events.

This simple act of writing down your feelings will help you better understand your emotions, which will help you express what you're going through in a way that allows your partner to see the situation from your point of view.

When you feel as if you've worked through your emotions and have nothing else to write down, read over what you've written. Did you miss anything? If so, keep writing. The length of this process varies from person to person. When you feel like you have no more emotions to convey, sit with your feelings for a while. It's helpful to fully feel and accept your emotions, rather than over- or underreact to them. Take the time to listen to your monitor—it will help you collect your thoughts.

Additional Advice for Dealing with Your Emotions Constructively

Honoring your emotions involves more than just acknowledging how you're feeling; it also entails making a commitment to act on your emotions in a manner that serves your interests. When dealing with an intimate betrayal, it can be wise to reflect on what's best for you and set goals accordingly.

Reflect on Your Goals. Setting goals can help you take the emotions you're experiencing and put them to good use. Identifying your goals also makes it easier for you to evaluate whether your actions are helping you get what you want.

After days of not speaking to Ethan about his sexting with a coworker, Hannah felt lost. She was thinking, "How's this going to help?" Because she was so upset, it took her a while, but she ultimately realized that she needed to get to the bottom of what happened. She wanted to know the truth. Once Hannah decided what she absolutely needed from Ethan, she was able to take her anger and think about ways that she could get him to be honest with her. Yelling at her husband wasn't working, so she started thinking through her options. Ultimately, she decided to tell Ethan, "I'm so frustrated right now; the only thing that will help me is knowing the truth, however painful it might be."

When you're feeling overwhelmed or out of control, it can be hard to set goals. However, when people don't have a clear outcome in mind, they're more likely to act out in unhelpful (and sometimes contradictory) ways. If Hannah hadn't taken the time to consider her goals, she might have continued not speaking to Ethan or kept up her attacks on him, which would have gotten her nowhere.

Because it's so easy to lose sight of your goals in a crisis, we have designed the following activity to help you. Grab a pen and something to write on. It helps to do this activity by hand (not on a keyboard). Given the betrayal you experienced, reflect on your immediate goals. Do you want to know the truth? Do you want to understand why your partner betrayed your trust? Do you want to know if the problem can be fixed? Do you want your partner to acknowledge the pain they have caused? Again, it's useful to write down what you want to accomplish. Be as specific and clear as possible.

Once you have your list, reflect on how you would prioritize your goals. Which ones are the most important to you? After you've prioritized your goals, write them down in order of importance. However, this time around, also write down *why* you want to accomplish each particular goal. Elaborate in as much detail as possible why each goal is important to you. For example, if one of your goals is to get to the bottom of what happened, why is that one of your top priorities? Will knowing the truth make your uncertainty go away? Or will knowing the truth help you decide if your relationship can be saved? Take some time to think through why you want to accomplish each goal, and try to spell out your reasoning in detail.

Elaborating on your goals using this method can make it easier for you to keep your focus when talking with your partner. Whenever you're feeling lost, overwhelmed, or out of control, remember your goals and use them as guideposts to direct you where you want to go. When planning a road trip, you can't pick a route until you know your destination. The same is true when dealing with problems in relationships.

Borrowing an analogy from neuroscientist Sam Harris, who has written about the benefits of handling problems constructively, helps to highlight the importance of focusing on your goals in a time of crisis. Imagine that a pipe bursts in your house. You and your partner panic, yell, scream, and run around trying to figure out what to do. In the meantime, every second that passes leads to more water on the floor. Eventually, you get around to turning off the water and grabbing towels to clean up the mess. A lot of unnecessary energy was spent on freaking out when it could have been used to solve the problem. This is forgivable if it's the first time something like this happened. But if the pipe bursts again, you will have a clearer sense of what to do. Sure, you're upset, but the second time around, you will focus on what really matters and solve the problem more quickly and with less damage.

As Sam Harris notes, throughout life we can deal with problems effectively or get caught up in additional drama, which diverts our energy away from achieving our ultimate outcome. A constructive approach to dealing with an intimate betrayal is like dealing with a bursting pipe. You can learn to put your energy into strategies that help you quickly achieve your goals.

Turning to Others for Support

It may also help to reach out to others for support. Maybe there is someone in your life who is good at letting you vent. This may be someone who has helped you with past relational problems. Before discussing your current situation, keep in mind that when dealing with an intimate betrayal, other people's responses may not be all that helpful. While a friend's response probably comes from a place of protectiveness, he or she doesn't have to live with the consequences and may not have the same concern you have about trying to save your relationship. Friends and family members often have different agendas than you do and may never forgive your partner, even if you're eventually able to.

For example, when Hannah finally decided to disclose what happened with Ethan to her mother, her mother told the rest of the family, and soon Hannah was inundated with advice (her mother begged her to move out), hostility (her older sister told her she was being typically hysterical and ruining a good relationship; her younger sister said she'd never liked Ethan in the first place), and even threats (her father threatened to harm Ethan).

So if you feel like reaching out to someone, think through that decision carefully. Specifically, reach out to a friend, therapist, or spiritual leader who will remain nonjudgmental. You may be thinking, "Who could remain nonjudgmental at a time like this?" While that's a valid point, asking this question can help you narrow the list of people who will help you to reflect on your emotions rather than try to impose their own solution to your problem. Hopefully, you have a friend who has been nonjudgmental in the past and will validate your feelings rather than give you advice. If you don't have a nonjudgmental friend, and journaling or our website isn't working for you, seeing a counselor may best help you work through this process.

Putting It All Together

When a crisis hits, it's easy for us to let our emotions get the best of us. However, when dealing with an intimate betrayal, our emotional reactions can sometimes cause more harm than good. When people honor their emotions and set clear goals, they have an easier time working with their partner to repair the harm done.

Takeaways

- Intimate betrayals trigger intense emotional reactions.
- Explosive and dismissive emotional reactions, while common, are counterproductive when trying to work through problems and restore trust.
- Learning how to honor your emotions can help calm you down, collect your thoughts, and approach problems in a way that is more likely to gain your partner's cooperation.
- When you're upset, setting goals can also help you use your emotions to your advantage.
- When reaching out to others for support, turn to someone who will listen to you and not interfere in the situation.

CHAPTER 7

———

(Re)Engaging Your Partner Constructively

To RESOLVE AN intimate betrayal in a meaningful way, you will need your partner's willingness and cooperation. The best way to gain your partner's cooperation is to get him or her to see the situation from your point of view.

Although extremely difficult, it can help to put yourself in your partner's shoes for just a minute. Imagine that you've betrayed your partner in a horrible way. How would you like your partner to raise the issue with you?

Remember Brian and Ashley? Brian was understandably devastated when he received a Facebook message from a stranger who claimed to be sleeping with his girlfriend. When he finally had a chance to talk to Ashley face-to-face about it, the conversation did not go over well. He immediately accused her, asked a lot of direct questions, and demanded to be told the truth: "Did you cheat on me? Who is he? How do you know him? You better tell me exactly what happened!"

While it's very easy to understand Brian's perspective, it also helps to see the conversation from Ashley's point of view. Although it can be hard to do in moments like this, viewing the confrontation from your partner's perspective will make you less likely to communicate in ways that prevent you from achieving your goals. You're going to need to gain your partner's cooperation. But that's virtually impossible when a pattern of accusations and defensiveness sets in.

Seasoned interrogators intuitively understand the relationship between asking pointed questions and deception. What is the first rule of interrogating a suspect? Never ask an accusatory question (despite the TV detectives who ask, "Why did you...?"). Asking direct questions puts the listener on the spot and makes getting the truth more difficult. Innocent or not, most people don't like to be accused of anything, much less an intimate betrayal. When placed in a confrontational setting, many people shift into some combination of a fight/flight/freeze response; they attack back, conceal the truth or lie, or say nothing. People are wired to protect themselves.

If you want to get results, do what the experts do. Try to create empathy between you and your partner rather than be viewed as an opponent. And the best way to do that is to share your emotions. Notice we said *share* your emotions, not *show* your emotions. It's important to honor your emotions, but you should not let them interfere with clear, direct communication. By articulating your thoughts and feelings to your partner—just like you did to yourself in the exercise from the last chapter—you allow them to understand what you're going through. If you can get your partner to see the betrayal from your point of view, he or she will be more likely to work with you to make amends.

Setting the Conditions for Cooperative Communication

For any serious discussion involving your relationship, there are a few practical factors to take into consideration. It's best to have difficult conversations earlier in the day, rather than later, because people are better able to exercise self-control, show empathy, and be considerate when they are not fatigued. Many discussions spiral into arguments in the evening because couples are often too tired, cranky, and worn-out to have a serious conversation.

Furthermore, sensitive issues are best addressed in a private setting where both people feel comfortable. Pick a setting that is on neutral turf and where both parties can easily leave if need be. Bringing your partner to *your* therapist may not feel like neutral turf. And showing up at your partner's place of work unannounced isn't going to work in your favor.

Plan to set aside a lot of time for such discussions; they often last longer than you think. And choose a time when both of you are not feeling rushed or have other things to attend to. For instance, bringing up an intimate betrayal while dealing with a sick child, or when one of you has a pressing deadline at work, is not ideal. And avoiding alcohol is always a good idea.

If you've already confronted your partner and it didn't go over well, definitely take the time, setting, and location into account when bringing up the issue again.

Create Empathy. Once you've decided on the appropriate time and place, the best way to get a partner to understand how you have been hurt is to explain how you're feeling. Don't attack (assign blame), ask a ton of questions (create a defensive environment), or try to impose a solution (control the outcome)—don't tell your partner exactly what they must do to fix the problem ("I want you to never talk to her again!"). Simply explain that you're feeling sad, hurt, fearful, whatever. Try to focus on emotional terms, many of which we listed in Chapter 6, that best capture your feelings and are likely to create an empathetic response.

Saying "I'm so *angry*" is far less effective than saying "I'm so *hurt.*" While both words describe what being betrayed feels like, *hurt* has a better chance of being heard. Always go with the phrase that's both truthful *and* has the best chance of getting your partner to understand your point of view. Avoid using words that cast judgment on your partner. Instead, focus on words that highlight your distress. Here are some examples of how emotions can be expressed in ways that produce empathy:

Emotional Expression	Empathetic Expression
I am so *pissed off.*	I'm so *hurt.*
How could you *betray* me?	I'm *confused* about how and why this happened.
You're so *rude and inconsiderate.*	I'm so *sad.*
You *destroyed* my life.	I'm *uncertain* about our future.
You *humiliated* me.	I'm feeling *embarrassed.*
I'm so *disgusted* by what you did.	I'm *taken aback* by what happened.

You make my *blood boil*.	I'm so full of *fear* right now.
You *irritate* me.	I'm feeling *overwhelmed*.

Can you see how the left column describes feelings and casts judgment on a partner? The right column communicates your feelings without assigning blame. Also pay close attention to the tone of your voice. If your tone conveys anger and hostility, rather than sadness and fear, the conversation is likely to turn into an argument, no matter what words you say.

When Brian confronted Ashley, not only did he use accusatory language ("Did you cheat on me?") but also the tone of his voice conveyed hostility. And Ashley did what many people do in such situations—she lied. She said that she would never cheat on him—that she would never do that to him. Only when Brian confronted her with concrete evidence did Ashley break down. She started crying and said she was sorry. She promised never to cheat on him again. Brian was enraged! Ashley cheated on him, lied about it, and *now* wanted him to forgive her? A major fight ensued. By the end of the evening, not only

Example of a Counterproductive Conversation Using Accusations

She: "I'm so mad you talked to your ex after you promised not to."

He: "I didn't reach out to her, she reached out to me."

She: "But you promised not to talk to her!"

He: "I was just being polite."

She: "Oh, so you care more about her feelings than mine!"

did Brian feel misunderstood, he wasn't sure he could work things out with Ashley. In fact, the next morning he decided to move out.

What if Brian had taken a different path? If Brian had reflected on his emotions about being betrayed and tried to share them in a way that created empathy, things might have turned out differently. Let's be honest, no matter what, the conversation between Brian and Ashley would have been gut-wrenchingly painful. However, if he could have approached her in a way that prevented the likelihood of her lying about what happened, it would have been helpful. For example, if Brian started the conversation by saying, "Ashley, I love you, and I really care about our relationship. I want to talk about what happened. I'm so hurt, confused, and sad," fewer lies might have been told, less damage would have been done to their relationship, and the issues to address would have been put on the table.

Again, we understand the urge to vent or punish a partner can be strong. And we know that some of your family and friends may advise you to put your partner in their place—to avoid coming across as being weak. However, it takes real wisdom and strength to approach relationship problems with a constructive mind-set—and it works better.

Start the conversation by expressing your feelings. Try not to argue or bicker over what really happened or didn't happen. Although you probably don't know all of the details and have a lot of unanswered questions, it helps if you can begin the process by creating a sense of empathy between you and your partner. The more your partner can empathize with you, the more likely you'll be to find out the truth and reach a satisfying solution.

Example of a Productive Conversation Using Empathy

She: "I'm sad, and I want to explain how I'm feeling."

He: "What's going on?"

She: "I felt hurt when I found out you talked to her. I don't want to get into the details; I just want you to know how I'm feeling."

He: "She reached out to me. I was just trying to be polite."

She: "I really need you to listen to how I'm feeling right now. We can get into the details later, but I'll feel better if you try to listen to how I'm feeling."

He: "OK, I'm listening."

Reading a Partner's Response

Once you begin the conversation, you will also need to monitor your partner's response. Research consistently shows that how your partner acts or reacts in times of disagreement, conflict, or distress determines whether you should remain together and can be happy as a couple.

Cooperative Response. When you express your feelings constructively, there are three things you should look for in your partner's response.

- Does your partner make the effort to listen to what you have to say?
- Does he or she validate your point of view?
- Does he or she show concern for how you're feeling?

If you answer yes to these questions, your partner is probably doing his or her best to listen to you, and that's a good sign. You can also determine if your partner is being responsive by simply asking yourself if you feel understood, validated, and cared for when expressing your feelings. If you do, then things are headed in the right direction.

Dismissive Response. If your partner is dismissive and shuts down or stops listening, take note of it. Most people are good at noticing when a partner isn't responding to their concerns in an empathetic way, but few know what to do when it happens. Don't immediately respond to their indifferent reaction with accusatory or negative expressions—that would negate all the effort you've put into dealing with the issue constructively. There's a difference between noting how people behave and *reacting* to how they behave.

If your partner is dismissing your feelings, you might also be tempted to try to force them to be present. During some of their conversations, George had a hard time listening to Maria talk about how devastated she felt because of his affair. He would get a blank, distant look on his face, as if he were somewhere else. This drove Maria crazy, and she would sometimes scream, "Pay attention to what I'm saying!"

Instead, it would have been better for her to express her frustration by saying, "I'm sad and confused because I don't feel understood," but not push it too far. People who have a tendency to "check out"—typically people with a cool style of attachment—often completely do so when forced to listen. If you consistently run into a brick wall when trying to get your partner to empathize with you, the problem you're dealing with is probably larger than the betrayal you uncovered, so talking with a counselor may be your best option.

Defensive Response. If your partner gets defensive or wants to argue about what happened, avoid going down that path. Tell him or her that you just want to share your feelings and you can worry about the details or other issues later. Be explicit and say, "I just want to feel understood right now." If you feel yourself getting frustrated or agitated, come back to the phrase, "I just want to share my feelings; we'll talk about details later." If your partner *still* responds defensively, take a break and make it clear that you don't want to move forward until you've expressed your feelings and have been heard. Don't let the conversation stray into other issues or topics.

When Maria first confronted George about his affair, she accused him of humiliating her and ruining her life. George got defensive, lied about the affair, and told Maria that she was crazy. A similar pattern occurred with Hannah and Ethan, when she accused him of sexting with Stephanie. Again, he said it wasn't a big deal—that she was taking the conversation out of context—it was just the way he and Stephanie liked to joke around (when, in fact, he had strong feelings for Stephanie). He also accused Hannah of snooping on him and said he was shocked that she didn't love him enough to trust him. Ethan actually said *he* felt betrayed by *her* actions and accusations.

Another way your partner might become defensive is by turning the conversation back to you and your behavior or dredging up mistakes you've made in the past. Or they may try to bring up your role in events that led to the betrayal (for example, "I did what I did because of what you did years ago"). If this happens, don't take the bait. Try to steer the conversation back to what you're feeling and the transgression at hand. Other issues can be addressed later, but right now it's important to focus on the current problem and to try to get your partner to acknowledge how you're feeling about being betrayed.

Again, take a break if you have to, but when you resume, be sure to focus on your emotions before addressing other issues. The issues can wait until you've established a cooperative pattern of interaction—one where your partner listens to your point of view. If he or she constantly refuses to listen to you, the problem isn't likely to be resolved, and tough decisions, like ending the relationship, should be considered.

Remember Adam and his wife, Nadine, who spent a thousand dollars on a wedding gift? Let's imagine that Adam adopted a constructive approach when raising the issue with his wife. The following examples illustrate what a cooperative, dismissive, and defensive response from a partner might look like.

Cooperative Response from a Partner

Adam: "I wanted to bring something up. Something's bothering me. I found out how much money was spent on the wedding gift. I'm disappointed, and I want to talk about it."

Nadine: "OK, let's talk."

Adam: "I'm confused and disappointed over the cost of the wedding gift. I want you to know where I'm coming from."

Nadine: "I get it. I spent way too much."

Dismissive Response from a Partner

Adam: "I wanted to bring something up. Something's
        bothering me. I found out how much money
        was spent on the wedding gift. I'm disappoint-
        ed, and I want to talk about it."

Nadine: "Really! Do we have to talk about this?"

Adam: "I would just like you to consider the situation
        from my perspective."

Nadine: "It's done already. I don't see the point in argu-
        ing about this."

Adam: "I'm frustrated that we can't talk about this."

Defensive Response from a Partner

Adam: "I wanted to bring something up. Something's
        bothering me. I found out how much money
        was spent on the wedding gift. I'm disappoint-
        ed, and I want to talk about it."

Nadine: "I wanted to get them something special—it's
        only money, and you've spent just as much on
        stupid stuff over the years."

Adam: "We can talk about all of that later. Right now, I
        just want you to understand where I'm coming
        from."

Ideally, your goal is to get your partner to listen to what you have to say and empathize with your point of view. If you can't gain your partner's cooperation, the odds of working things out are virtually nonexistent. While it only takes one person's mistakes to bring a relationship crashing down, it requires both parties' cooperation to make things right. You cannot rebuild trust on your own.

Additional Activities to Help You Engage Your Partner Constructively

These two activities are helpful when couples need to have a difficult, uncomfortable conversation.

Outsider's Perspective. Approaching your partner with a constructive mind-set is easier to do when you take a moment to see the situation from a different viewpoint. Imagine that you weren't involved in the betrayal at hand. How would you recommend that someone else bring up the issue with their partner? Spend five minutes writing down how you think someone else should raise the issue and handle the problem. Be specific. What exactly should that person say to their partner? Also consider that person's nonverbal behavior. Would you recommend that the person raise the issue calmly or with a lot of anger and hostility?

Even people who have made a serious mistake and caused considerable harm to a partner want to be treated with respect. By treating your partner in a respectful, thoughtful manner, you're more likely to gain their cooperation. We aren't saying that gaining your partner's cooperation will solve all of your problems, but without it, there's little point in going forward. The sooner you adopt a constructive approach, the sooner you'll discover if the two of you can fix what's broken. Viewing the situation from an outsider's perspective, even for a moment, can help you find a better way to approach your partner with your concerns.

Reflect on a Positive Experience. This next activity works best if you do it right before you start the conversation with your partner. Take a few moments to think about a time when you and your partner were able to discuss and resolve a problem in your relationship—a discussion where your partner made you feel understood and worked with you to successfully deal with the issue at hand. Try to recall as many details of this encounter as you can, especially how you felt when your partner was responsive to your needs and concerns. Recalling such instances *immediately* before talking to your partner can provide you with some reassurance that the two of you can handle difficult conversations constructively—you've done it before.

Advice for the Betrayer

When your partner is describing how the betrayal made him or her feel, do your best to validate your partner's feelings. Your partner's feelings are genuine and need to be acknowledged. Be explicit. Tell your partner you understand how he or she feels. "You're angry, mad, and disappointed. You have every right to be." This is not the time to get into discussions about the facts and details of what happened or try to explain your side of the story (that comes later). Right now, your partner needs to know that you get what they're going through.

After weeks of giving George the silent treatment, Maria decided she needed to have an honest discussion about what happened, if there was even a slight chance of saving their marriage. This time around, Maria was able to tell George exactly how she felt—hurt, sad, and confused.

Although George struggled to listen to Maria, given his cool style of attachment, he knew he had too much at stake not to. He wanted to save his family, marriage, and business. Though he fumbled at first, he was ultimately able to acknowledge his wife's pain by saying, "I've hurt you beyond belief." That simple acknowledgment brought much needed relief to Maria. Everyone has a fundamental need to be understood. It's the cornerstone of reestablishing a sense of trust between partners.

After moving out, Brian missed Ashley and wanted to talk about what happened. This time around, he started the conversation by telling Ashley that he was feeling hurt, sad, and disappointed. Initially, Ashley started apologizing profusely, but Brian stopped her and asked her to just hear him out. He said that he wanted her to understand how he was feeling. Again, she started apologizing, and Brian finally told her, "Please stop. Just listen to me. I need you to understand what I'm going through." It took her a while, but Ashley finally managed to tell Brian what he needed to hear. She told him, "I get it. You're angry because I hurt you in the worst way possible."

Hannah and Ethan had a more difficult time. Because Hannah had a hard time controlling her emotions and staying focused on the main issue—Ethan sexting with Stephanie—he had a difficult time listening to her, and he eventually tuned Hannah out. Both Hannah and Ethan are trapped in a state of accusations and denials—definitely not on the path to recovery.

In Zachary and Jacob's case, Zachary had a difficult time explaining how he felt about Jacob looking for a job and how he felt it would undermine their relationship. Rather than explain his feelings, Zachary told Jacob,

"You don't care about me." Because Zachary leveled an accusation, Jacob got defensive and shot back, "I would have told you the truth, but you make it impossible to do." Clearly, this relationship is nearing its end.

When trying to rebuild trust, it's critical for the betrayer to make the betrayed partner feel understood, or the entire conversation will go nowhere (or the conversation will go around in circles until the betrayed partner finally feels validated). People who have been betrayed have a difficult time moving forward until they know that their partner understands what they are experiencing. It's really that simple.

Putting It All Together

Following the discovery of a transgression or betrayal, focusing on your feelings and expressing yourself in a nonjudgmental way is helpful for several reasons. You're less likely to create a defensive response—a response where emotions escalate, more lies are told, and conversations turn into heated arguments. The more you can move away from triggering a defensive response, the more likely you are to motivate your partner to see the situation from your point of view and get to the root of the problem with less drama and negativity. The quicker you adopt a constructive approach, the more likely you'll be to start an open, honest dialogue with your partner about the transgression that occurred and make it possible for you to work toward reconciliation. It's also essential for the person who betrayed their partner's trust to acknowledge the harm that's been done.

Takeaways

- The best way to convey to your partner how you're feeling is to create empathy and avoid blame.
- The best way to get your partner to listen to you is to express your feelings in a nonconfrontational way.
- Stick to your plan and don't let your partner derail your ability to express yourself.
- Pay close attention to your partner's reaction when expressing your feelings.

CHAPTER 8

Resolving the Issue and Rebuilding Trust—Part I

F YOU'RE ABLE to have a constructive exchange with your partner—one in which your partner can listen and acknowledge what you have to say—we've designed an eight-step process that will help the two of you resolve the issue and rebuild trust. Because betrayals have a common structure, they also have a common solution. Although the specific details vary based on the nature of the betrayal you experienced, the basic process involved in building trust is the same.

We'll help you work through the steps involved. In doing so, we've intentionally kept our advice straightforward and to the point. While our presentation is simple, however, the process is far from simple or easy. Rebuilding trust requires a great deal of patience, understanding, and cooperation. As we lay out a road map of the conversations you'll need to have with your partner, we know that you'll probably run into obstacles unique to your specific situation. It's our hope that you'll participate in the online community through the website that accompanies this book (www.brokentrust.com) to find solutions to the specific challenges that emerge depending on the details of the betrayal you've encountered.

Listed here is an overview of the various steps involved in rebuilding trust. We'll work through what both you and your partner need to do in every step of this process in this chapter and the next.

Steps to Rebuild Trust

1. Describe the Transgression
2. Clarify the Facts
3. Make/Accept Sincere Apologies
4. Explain the Reason for the Betrayal
5. Create a Plan
6. Stick to Your Plan
7. Assess Your Progress
8. Be Patient

To begin, three key actions need to happen next in order to save your relationship: both partners need to discuss the transgression, what happened needs to be clarified, and the person who betrayed their partner's trust needs to apologize for their actions. It's not critical that these steps happen in this exact order. Most of the time, an apology works best after the responsible party owns up to the facts of the betrayal. Sometimes apologies can be blended into the discussion of what happened. It really depends on what feels right, given your circumstances.

Before we get into the specifics about the first three steps in the process of rebuilding trust, we must emphasize that being honest with each other is absolutely critical. Both *telling* and *hearing* the truth are necessary when trying to reestablish a genuine connection between you and your partner. *It's through the process of sharing information, listening to each other, and creating solutions together that couples learn to trust each other again.*

The process of rebuilding trust won't be fun or easy. It's like passing a hot potato back and forth. Holding a hot potato in your hand isn't enjoyable—it hurts. If you take a step back and look at the situation from a distance, passing a potato between two people requires a lot of cooperation; you can't pass a hot potato by yourself. Discussing difficult topics, like holding the hot potato, is unavoidable. Cooperating with your partner without giving up on passing the hot potato back and forth is the real goal.

Having honest discussions with your partner about an intimate betrayal is sure to trigger intense emotional reactions. When you're feeling overwhelmed or you reach what feels like an impasse, try to do the following:

- Acknowledge and honor your emotions.
- Reflect on the goals you hope to accomplish.
- Take your partner's perspective into account.

If you slip up and fall into old, counterproductive patterns—such as yelling, blaming, or shaming—cut yourself some slack. You and your partner are bound to make mistakes during this process. What's important is that you become aware of your slipups and get back on track as quickly as you can.

As you and your partner go through this process, it also helps if you can adopt the following mind-set: you both are on the same side. *It's the two of you against the problems you face, not you against one another.*

Rebuilding Trust Activity

Research shows that, as couples work through a betrayal, they are more likely to be successful when they're able to take a few moments to reflect on the positive aspects of the transgression that came to light. Yes, you read that correctly—every betrayal can have some positive outcomes. Indeed, every negative event you encounter is an opportunity to gain new information, learn, and grow.

To find out how, write down the positive things that have come from the harm your partner caused you. Maybe you discovered you're stronger than you thought you were. Or maybe you've gained potentially long-lasting wisdom and insights that will help you in the future. Perhaps the betrayal is forcing you to discuss important issues in your relationship that you were hesitant to address. It's possible that you now have a better understanding of exactly what you need and expect from a partner in order to feel safe, loved, and cared for. Try to reflect deeply on the positive things that have come about and write them down.

As you and your partner work through the process of rebuilding trust, it's common to get sidetracked on issues that aren't relevant to the betrayal you experienced. If that happens, use the steps for rebuilding trust as a guide to getting your discussions back on track.

Step 1: Describe the Transgression

Betrayed Partner

Once you're able to engage your partner constructively, it's necessary to talk about what happened. If you've been betrayed, describe to your partner how he or she violated your trust. Be specific about how your partner's actions violated your expectations. When describing how your partner betrayed you, do your best to use descriptive rather than evaluative language. Descriptive language specifies what happened in a relatively neutral way, while evaluative language is overly critical and judgmental.

When Maria and George started talking about the betrayal, she was descriptive and to the point, "I assumed you'd be faithful to me, and I now know you had a long-term affair with Teresa." Maria could have used more evaluative language and said, "I assumed you'd be faithful, but you went behind my back and cheated on me." Using evaluative language is more likely to create a defensive response from a partner, which prevents couples from having productive conversations.

Hannah struggled to use descriptive language when telling Ethan why she was upset and accused him of "flirting" with someone from work. Using the word *flirting*, while probably accurate, is an emotionally charged way of describing the problem. It would have been better had Hannah said, "I didn't expect you would exchange sexually suggestive messages with someone else, but you did." Again, the more you can describe what happened without focusing on a partner's intentions or the outcome of what happened, the easier it will be to talk about the betrayal.

Zachary struggled even more. Rather than talking about how Jacob violated his expectations by applying for jobs on the opposite coast (descriptive), Zachary told Jacob, "You fooled me into thinking you wanted to be with me!" to which Jacob replied, "I knew you'd overreact" (an accusation followed by a defensive response).

If you're having a hard time coming up with a descriptive way to discuss the problem, think about how you would like your partner to address the issue with you. It also helps to focus on the key facts of the immediate betrayal rather than elaborate on every single detail of what transpired. Focusing on the key facts makes it easier for your partner to hear you out.

When Brian started to talk about why he was so upset with Ashley, he did a good job of using descriptive language and focused on the main issue: "I was really hurt when I found out you slept with someone else," rather than overwhelming her with everything he knew.

Finally, it also helps to try to remain as calm as possible. Pay close attention to your nonverbal behavior and the tone of your voice. Try not to let your hostility or anger show. The more you can talk about the details of what happened in a calm, direct manner, the better.

Repairing Betrayed Partner's Trust

If you're the betrayer, it's critical to admit the facts of what you did. Denying the truth or withholding information will only make things worse in the long run. If your partner describes how you actually behaved, admit it. Owning up to the basic facts demonstrates your willingness to be cooperative and take responsibility for your actions. This isn't the time to offer long apologies, make excuses, or engage in other attempts to explain your behavior. This is the moment to simply say, "Yes, I did that."

When Maria told George what she knew about his affair, he struggled. He just wanted to focus on their future, not on his mistakes; but he also knew he had to come clean and say, "I hate admitting it, but it's true." Again, depending on the circumstances, this might also be a good time to offer a simple apology ("I'm sorry").

If your partner gets some of the facts wrong, don't point it out right away. First, take responsibility for what you did do. Your partner *needs* to hear you accept responsibility for your actions. You can clarify the details later. If your partner is hurling broad accusations at you, try to help him or her describe how your behavior violated their trust. Ask, "Can we talk about what I did that upset you, not what a terrible person I am?"

We know it can be difficult to hear someone pointing out mistakes you've made. It can bring out feelings of shame and inadequacy. If that happens, tell your partner you need a moment. Try not to let feelings of shame get in the way of admitting what you did. The sooner you take responsibility for what happened by admitting to the basic facts involved, the sooner you'll be able to talk about your perspective or the issues you want to raise. It's all a matter of timing. You need to listen and validate your partner now, so they will be more open to listening to you later—it's through this collaborative process where couples talk to each other in considerate and respectful ways that trust is slowly regained.

When Brian tried to talk about how Ashley betrayed him, she wanted to explain her actions, rather than simply owning up to the facts. She told him, "I never meant to hurt you." This frustrated Brian; he didn't feel as if she was taking responsibility for what she had done. Brian finally asked her to just fess up and stop making excuses, which she eventually did. Don't force your partner to make you take responsibility for your actions. It doesn't demonstrate a willingness to be cooperative or make things right. There is a time to explain your side of the story, but you need to acknowledge your mistakes first.

When people have been hurt, they want to know that their partner not only understands them but also acknowledges what they did. George had an affair. Ashley slept with someone else. Ethan exchanged sexual text messages with a coworker. And Jacob applied for jobs on the West Coast. All of these things happened, and the events need to be acknowledged. As difficult as it may be to discuss the basic facts of what transpired, such honest conversations are part of the process of rebuilding trust.

Step 2: Clarify the Facts

When a betrayal comes to light, the person who has been betrayed typically knows some of the details, but not all of the facts. Maria knew that George had been cheating on her, but she didn't know the extent to which he was involved with Teresa. Was George in love with Teresa? Was he thinking about ending their marriage? Brian knew some of what happened between Ashley and Alex, but he had questions he wanted answered. How long had their affair been going on? Did they ever have sex in their bed?

After couples agree on the basic details, most of the time the betrayed partner wants to know more: "I need to know exactly what happened." Seeking out the facts, while painful to hear, can help reduce uncertainty and doubt. When people don't know the basic facts involved, it can become hard to move beyond the betrayal that occurred. People's imaginations may run wild. We are not saying that every sordid detail needs to be discussed—this can actually cause unnecessary emotional trauma—but the basic outline of what happened needs to be made clear. Questions and doubts may linger, fostering suspicions and anxiety, unless the betrayed partner's questions are put to rest once and for all.

Betrayed Partner

When seeking out the facts, we strongly advise against snooping on a partner. Snooping is a violation of a partner's privacy, which can further erode trust among couples. Snooping is also likely to increase the snooper's anxiety because it's very easy to take information out of context and interpret it in the worst possible way.

For example, Maria went through all George's phone records, but she had a difficult time determining what to make of calls to unknown numbers. Maria's snooping actually left her feeling more uncertain about the extent of George's cheating. Was the affair with Teresa a one-time mistake or a larger pattern of behavior? The best way to deal with these feelings of doubt and uncertainty is to ask a partner for the facts you want. Asking questions is ethical, can lead to honest conversations, and helps restore trust. Snooping rarely helps couples feel closer and more connected.

If you have questions about what happened, ask them. It's important that you get the information *you* want, but try to focus on the basics of what happened and not on every minute detail, which can cause more pain and trauma. Knowing the basic facts of what transpired can help reduce your suspicions and uncertainty and be useful when trying to develop solutions.

It's also important to set some limits on the information being sought. Do your best to focus on the fundamental issues, rather than on the smallest of details. For example, if your partner had an affair, it's important to know how it started, how long it lasted, and how involved the relationship was. It's not helpful to know what nicknames they may have called each other, what restaurants they went to, what table they sat at, and other small details. Asking about the smallest of details can prolong the process, and it doesn't help address the important facts. In fact, seeking out the minute details of what happened can take quite a bit of time that might otherwise be used in healthier ways. When you focus your questions on the fundamental facts involved, you're more likely to identify solutions to prevent it from happening again.

While getting to the basic facts of what happened will reduce your uncertainty, the things your partner tells you are going to be very difficult to hear. When your partner answers your questions, do your best to listen and avoid reacting in hostile ways. If you're experiencing intense emotions, take a break and reflect on how you're feeling. You should express how you feel, but don't take your negative feelings out on your partner.

If you don't want to know more than what you already know, that's your right. But keep this in mind: if other details come to light later, it will be difficult for you to blame your partner for not bringing it up. While you may not want to hear more details now, it may be in your best interest to get the key issues out in the open. Knowing the truth, however painful, will help you evaluate the situation and find potential solutions.

Repairing Betrayed Partner's Trust

When your partner asks what happened, tell the truth. This isn't the time to omit details, conceal facts, or lie. If these questions are not answered honestly, suspicions will linger, and the truth will probably come out anyway. Telling the truth can be difficult and awkward, because you probably don't want to hurt or upset your partner more than you already have, but putting the facts on the table is part of the healing process.

It may help to keep in mind that your partner is entitled to the truth. He or she deserves to have his or her questions answered. You and your partner are trying to build a life together; telling the truth is part of the deal. When your partner is asking for details, focus on the facts. Do your best not to offer excuses—just describe what happened. While you don't want to hurt your partner more than you already have, concealing facts or trying to justify your actions is going to cause more problems. There is a time to tell your side of the story, but this is not that moment. When your partner is asking for the truth, this is your opportunity to show you can be trusted—by being honest.

Maria had many questions. She wanted to know exactly how and when the affair started as well as the basics of what transpired both sexually and emotionally. She also wanted to know if there were other women in his life. George hated having this conversation. Sometimes he wanted to give short, blunt answers: "Yes, we had a lot of sex." And he also found himself wanting to tell Maria more than she wanted to know. "Many women are attracted to me," he bragged. Although it took a long time, and many discussions, George was ultimately able to answer his wife's questions in a factual, direct manner. George had had three affairs over the course of their marriage.

Brian wanted to know exactly who the other guy was. How did he and Ashley meet? Where and when did they hook up? Was he attractive? Ashley struggled to respond; she didn't want to hurt Brian's feelings. She really didn't want to tell Brian everything, especially the fact that Alex was extremely handsome. But realizing she had to come clean, she told the truth.

Hannah wanted to know if Ethan had sexual feelings for Stephanie. Because he had already lied to her and didn't want to have this conversation, he stuck to his original story and accused Hannah of being her typical self—an overreactor.

And Zachary wanted to know what else Jacob had been hiding from him. Jacob just shook his head in a sign of frustration. When a partner refuses to cooperate, it tells you everything you need to know.

The betrayed partner is entitled to the truth about what happened. Hearing the truth isn't easy, but telling the truth demonstrates that the party who is at fault is being cooperative and honest. Such conversations also help get the basic details out in the open, which reduces uncertainty about what happened. Knowing the truth is also useful because it serves as the foundation for identifying solutions to the problem at hand.

Step 3: Make/Accept Sincere Apologies

Sincere is the operative word here. Some people robotically say, "I'm sorry," and it ends up sounding fake. People often apologize hastily in order to get out of trouble without addressing the problem. In many circumstances, saying "I'm sorry" before validating a partner's feelings and owning up to the facts can give the appearance of being more concerned about ending a difficult conversation than about trying to address the issues.

An apology is much more likely to be effective (and accepted) when the betrayed individual's feelings have been acknowledged and the betrayer has taken responsibility for their actions by admitting to what they did.

Betrayed Partner

If your partner apologizes, listen to your partner and resist the temptation to immediately ask, "Why did you do this to me?" First, acknowledge the fact that your partner took ownership for the harm he or she caused you. Rebuilding trust requires both parties to acknowledge what the other person is saying. Take a moment to make your partner feel understood: "I needed to hear that."

After multiple conversations about the ways George had betrayed her, Maria needed some time to think things through. She wasn't sure that a future with him was possible. When the two got together to talk again, George started with an apology.

He said, "I'm so sorry for what happened. It's my fault."

"I appreciate hearing that," Maria replied.

Although they were talking about a painful experience, Maria somehow felt connected to George; she experienced a moment of intimacy with him. When two people take the time to listen and show each other respect, it creates a sense of closeness and trust, even when talking about difficult issues.

A similar outcome occurred when Ashley and Brian finished discussing the details of her sexual encounter with Alex.

"I'm sorry," admitted Ashley. "I really screwed things up."

Although Brian was extremely hurt, he felt the conversation was headed in the right direction and said, "Hearing that helps."

The situation between Hannah and Ethan was more complicated. Hannah didn't feel that Ethan had come clean about his sexting—he obviously exchanged provocative texts with Stephanie but denied that he had feelings for Stephanie. When Ethan said, "Trust me; it won't happen again," his words rang hollow. Somehow Hannah sensed that he wasn't being honest, sincere, or cooperative in trying to resolve the issue.

Zachary and Jacob didn't even get that far. The two of them are trapped in an endless cycle of accusations and defensiveness.

Repairing Betrayed Partner's Trust

A simple apology is generally the most effective. "I'm sorry. I messed up. It's my fault. I was wrong." Less is more here. Admit that you've harmed your partner and you regret what happened. Research shows that offering straightforward apologies leads to more forgiveness and less punishment. Avoid making excuses or offering explanations while apologizing. "I'm sorry, *but...*" diminishes the apology's effectiveness. Again, there is a time to offer an explanation or tell your side of the story, but it's important to let an apology stand on its own. Apologies seem less sincere when they are immediately followed by attempts to tell your side of the story.

The same goes with promising never to let it happen again. Making such promises, while often done to reassure a partner, isn't realistic. To begin with, if the betrayal happened once, it might happen again. Finding real solutions to problems requires a lot of work. Making promises never to do it again is too simplistic; it demonstrates a lack of seriousness about resolving the problem. Keeping your apology simple and to the point is the best way to go.

Putting It All Together

The first steps in rebuilding trust involve frank discussions, admissions of wrongdoing, and sincere apologies. The process works best when the person who has been betrayed can describe how their partner violated their expectations and the partner at fault takes responsibility for their actions, answers any questions truthfully, and apologizes for the harm they have done. Such conversations show a willingness to be cooperative and serve as the foundation for the next set of discussions, which are aimed at finding a solution to the issues that led to the problem in the first place.

Takeaways

- The betrayed individual needs to describe how their partner violated their expectations.
- The person who betrayed their partner's trust needs to be forthright about their shortcomings.
- The person who betrayed their partner's trust also needs to apologize for the damage their actions have caused.

CHAPTER 9

Resolving the Issue and Rebuilding Trust—Part II

W E HOPE YOU and your partner are able to implement the basic skills needed to talk about a serious issue with each other. Using the advice provided in the previous chapters, you and your partner should be able to honor and express your emotions, ask and answer questions in ways that prevent defensiveness, and show consideration and respect for each other. The skills you learned in the last chapter serve as the foundation for the next set of discussions that need to occur in order to work through the betrayal that happened and rebuild trust.

Step 4: Explain the Reason for the Betrayal

At this point, it's time for the person who was at fault to explain his or her side of the story and tell *why* the transgression occurred. Betrayals are complicated because even if people can agree on what happened (the details and facts), disagreements can arise over why the betrayal occurred in the first place.

It's important for the person who betrayed their partner's trust to have a chance to present his or her point of view. However, we can't stress the following enough: explanations should only be offered *after* feelings have been validated, the facts are out in the open, and sincere apologies have been given. Trying to offer explanations too soon won't help couples reestablish trust.

When a betrayed person has been *heard*, he or she is more likely to *listen* to a partner's side of the story. It's only through establishing a mutual understanding of what happened that couples can work on fixing problems and attempt to rebuild trust. Relationships are collaborative partnerships; it's important for both parties to describe their experiences and listen to each other.

Offering explanations allows couples to discuss the motivation underlying the betrayal, which serves as the basis for developing potential remedies, if any exist. As we've established throughout this book, betrayals often occur because of existing dynamics or patterns of behavior within a relationship; if those patterns are not uncovered, explained, and addressed, they can never be resolved, and the betrayal is likely to occur again.

Betrayed Partner

Listen to your partner's side of the story. While doing so, you're likely to experience negative emotions. Try to honor and express your feelings without resorting to personal attacks. If your negative feelings are getting in the way of acknowledging your partner's side of the story, be honest about it (you might say, "I'm having a hard time listening right now").

If you have questions about your partner's explanation, ask for more information. Your partner may not have all of the answers to your questions right away and may need some time to reflect before giving an answer.

If you hear flaws or inconsistencies in your partner's explanation, point them out. However, do it in a nonconfrontational way ("I'm a little confused. You said both X and Y and that doesn't make sense to me").

Just as your partner validated your perspective, you're going to have to acknowledge your partner's side of the story. You're going to have to understand what motivated your partner's behavior. You should be able to explain your partner's side of the story back to him or her. Understanding a partner's point of view, however, doesn't mean you agree with their position or condone their behavior. Understanding a partner's point of view simply means that you acknowledge what your partner felt and experienced at the time the betrayal occurred. It also helps to keep in mind that listening to a partner's perspective in no way diminishes or discounts your experience. You're entitled to your experiences just as your partner is entitled to theirs. Again, being able to work through differences is what distinguishes relationships that succeed from those that fail.

After Maria had time to contemplate the ways George had betrayed her, she wanted to know why he did it. George had a tough time explaining his behavior; he couldn't come up with a coherent explanation that made sense to him, let alone to his wife. This obviously didn't sit well with Maria, so she asked him to go to marital counseling with her, which he promptly agreed to.

After Ashley apologized to Brian, he wanted to understand why she cheated on him. She was embarrassed to tell him the truth; she was feeling lonely, and Alex gave her the attention she desired. It was difficult for Brian to hear that she cheated because she wasn't getting enough attention from him, but at least he had a better understanding of a major problem in their relationship.

While Hannah wanted to know why Ethan was sexting his coworker, Ethan continued to stick to his original story that he was just joking around, which left Hannah frustrated because Ethan never acknowledged her feelings or took responsibility for his actions.

Zachary and Jacob are out of the picture at this point. They're no closer to resolving their issues, and their relationship is in tatters.

At some point in the recovery process, the person who betrayed their partner's trust is going to have to provide an explanation for their behavior. It can be difficult for the person who's been betrayed to hear his or her partner's side of the story, but it's essential. It's difficult to solve problems when the underlying causes are not understood. Creating mutual understanding, even regarding painful issues, also fosters feelings of intimacy and closeness.

Repairing Betrayed Partner's Trust

When you've taken responsibility for your actions and acknowledged the harm you've caused, your partner is bound to ask for an explanation—"Why did you do it?" Now is the appropriate time to offer an explanation for your actions.

When explaining your actions, it helps if you understand the motivation underlying your behavior. If you're struggling to understand why you violated your partner's trust, it helps to focus on your feelings. What emotions were you experiencing when the betrayal occurred? If you can focus on what you were feeling, it can help identify what caused you to betray your partner's expectations. Perhaps your actions were motivated by anger, resentment, loneliness, not feeling in control of your life, the need for excitement, or something else. Again, our emotions alert us to issues that need to be addressed.

Focusing on the emotions underlying your betrayal can point out topics that are best solved through conversations with your partner. If you're struggling to identify what motivated your behavior, talking to a counselor is probably a wise course of action. Until you understand what motivated your behavior, this problem is likely to occur again.

When discussing the motives underlying your actions, it also helps to use descriptive rather than evaluative language. Again, descriptive language spells out what happened without assigning blame. Saying, "You *never* give me enough attention, I felt lonely, so I found someone who gave me the attention I needed," is not as effective as saying, "I felt lonely; someone gave me the attention I was seeking."

When you start talking about what motivated your behavior, your partner will undoubtedly have a lot of questions. Do your best to reflect on your feelings and motivation before answering your partner's questions. It's OK to ask for some time to think about why you behaved the way you did. Again, be honest with your partner about the reasons the betrayal occurred. It's only through honest discussions with a partner that intimacy and trust are restored.

Some people, especially those with a concerned style of attachment, have a tendency to engage in self-blame when they reflect on how they hurt their partners. Try to avoid falling into the trap of blaming yourself: "I'm such a horrible person." Feelings of self-blame prevent couples from finding solutions to their problems because when individuals engage in self-blame, they're essentially making themselves the problem. It's more helpful to reflect on how your feelings influenced your behavior—"My insecurities sometimes lead me to do things I regret." When people focus on how their feelings guided their actions, they're identifying a problem that can be solved—they need to find more constructive ways of dealing with their emotions.

Step 5: Create a Plan

It would be great to tell you the hard part is over, but it's not. Finding solutions to an intimate betrayal is not easy. Many couples take the easy route (and fail); they make promises they don't mean or can't keep. In many cases, both parties are going to have to make adjustments to their behavior in order to bring about lasting change. Effective solutions often require couples to develop plans where both partners implement new approaches and eliminate old ones. These plans should have the following characteristics:

Realistic. Let's face it—while minor transgressions can usually be readily resolved, major ones can't be fixed overnight. Like any major change in behavior, taking small steps is the best way to get there.

The plan your partner and you create should move you toward your ultimate goal, which we're assuming is to have a healthy, loving relationship. When developing such a plan, it helps to focus on small, realistic goals that can ultimately help you get your relationship back on track.

Although Ashley only cheated on Brian once, the problems in their relationship can't be solved anytime soon. Brian wants to be able to completely trust her again, and that's going to take a while. One of their immediate goals is to talk about their feelings *as they arise*; Ashley wants to talk about her insecurities when she feels the need, while Brian wants to discuss his lack of trust in Ashley whenever he feels like it. This small, initial plan is a step in the right direction.

Mutually Agreed Upon. Both partners must be committed to the plan for it to have any chance of success. The only way to achieve this is for you and your partner to develop your plan together. Discuss your expectations with each other and make sure you're on the same page. Remember, words can mean different things to different people. In Chapter 5, we gave advice for clarifying exactly what is meant—use descriptive language and confirm that your partner understands what you're saying ("Just to be clear, what did we agree to?").

You also need to work together to establish some ground rules to help you achieve your goals. For instance, Brian has specific ideas about what he wants Ashley to do: he wants her to delete Alex's contact information and switch to a new gym. Ashley also has suggestions for fixing their relationship: she wants to be able to share her feelings about not being appreciated; she wants Brian to be able to talk to her about his disappointment and lack of trust in her whenever he feels the need; and she wants them to spend some time together at least three times a week. By working together, they agreed on the following plan:

- Ashley would break off all contact with Alex.
- She would change gyms.

- She would discuss her insecurities rather than letting them get the best of her.
- Brian would discuss his feelings about what happened rather than bottling them up.
- They would check in with each other daily.
- They would spend at least three nights a week doing things they enjoyed as a couple including watching movies, going out to dinner, and attending sporting events.

Concrete and Verifiable. For any plan to have a chance of working, it needs to be both tangible and easily confirmable. Many couples fall into the trap of making plans that simply can't be proven or confirmed. For example, unless you lock your partner in the basement, promising never to cheat again is impossible to verify. However, all of the promises Brian and Ashley made can be observed, and therefore confirmed. Ashley gave Brian permission to check her email and phone records to make sure that Alex is out of the picture. Likewise, changing gyms is easy to verify. Sharing feelings with each other on a daily basis either happens or it doesn't. Seeing each other three times a week is certainly obvious. To rebuild trust, couples need to see that progress is being made—cooperation needs to be observed.

Both Partners

Work with your partner to create a realistic, concrete plan. Make your promises to each other explicit by putting them in writing. Again, words can mean different things to different people. Make sure that your partner and you are in agreement about the promises that have been made. Focusing on small, simple goals will make it easier for both of you to see immediate changes in your relationship, which will offer encouragement and hope that things are moving in the right direction.

Maria and George felt overwhelmed by the amount of issues they needed to address. Any couple in their situation would feel exactly the same way. With the help of a marital counselor, they decided to go slow and came up with the following plans:

- Attend couples counseling once a week.
- Behave professionally toward each other at work.
- Discuss feelings with each other at home on a daily basis.
- Have George sleep in the guest room until Maria feels comfortable sharing her bed with him again (if ever).

Step 6: Stick to Your Plan

This step should be fairly obvious, but it's important to emphasize: If you want to reestablish trust, you both have to keep your promises. No excuses, no explanations, just follow through. If you've betrayed your partner's trust and quickly break a promise again, you've compounded the problem. Don't drop the ball when it matters the most.

Both Partners

Stick to the plan you created with your partner. If you're struggling to stick to your plan, talk about it with your partner before mistakes are made. If you're feeling uncertain, insecure, or overwhelmed, be sure to discuss your feelings with your partner. Try your best to talk about issues as they arise.

At times, both Maria and George were stressed about the promises they made to each other. After a long day at work, coupled with their efforts to not let their issues spill over into their work and children's lives, they were exhausted. Because they were so wiped out during the week, they didn't feel like discussing their feelings. Rather than drop the ball, Maria explained how she felt—she was simply too tired to have a serious conversation at the end of a long day. George suggested that they have their daily talks in the morning.

When rebuilding trust, promises need to be kept. If you're struggling with the plan or agreements you made, discuss your feelings with your partner and try to find a reasonable alternative.

Step 7: Assess Your Progress

It's also important to set milestones. Depending on the issue you're trying to fix, you and your partner may wind up discussing issues on a daily basis. But it also helps to set aside a special time when you can evaluate your overall progress. Schedule a time together and put it in your calendar. Use this time to discuss the problems you've encountered while implementing your plan as well as note the progress you've made. You can do this once a month, every two months, or whenever you see fit.

During your assessments, if you realize you've made progress, celebrate it. Reward yourself for the work you've done. It's critically important to do something special together. Depending on your budget, interests, and imagination, try to do something together that you haven't done before. Go to a concert, have a picnic at the beach, or plan a weekend getaway. Doing something fun and novel is a great way of reestablishing intimacy and closeness. Having fun together also demonstrates a willingness to invest in each other—another way to demonstrate your commitment to making things better.

Both Partners

Plan specific times to talk with your partner about the problems you've encountered and the successes you've achieved and set new plans and goals. Do something fun and novel together to celebrate your achievements to date. Also, schedule another assessment and put it in your calendar.

After two months of sticking with their plan, Brian and Ashley talked about the headway they were making. Some problems came up: Ashley didn't always like sharing her insecurities with Brian because she didn't want to be a nuisance, and there were times when Brian's job was very demanding, which made it difficult for him to be fully engaged during their daily check-ins. With that said, they were feeling pretty good about their progress—they felt closer to each other, experienced more intimacy, and were beginning to think the relationship was getting back on track. To celebrate their success, they planned a hiking trip to Yosemite—something they always wanted to do. They also decided to increase their time together—from three to five times a week. Additionally, they planned on talking at least once a week about the possibility of Brian moving back in.

Step 8: Be Patient

When it comes to repairing trust, partners don't experience time in exactly the same way. If you're the person who was at fault and you're trying your best to fix the problem, you're keenly aware of everything you've done. As such, you probably feel that things are going well and are in a hurry to be forgiven.

Taking the perspective of the person who was betrayed, however, presents a different picture. People who have been betrayed have lost a sense of control over their lives. Regaining a sense of safety and rebuilding trust takes time. More importantly, it's up to the person who was betrayed to decide when things are improving and if and when forgiveness is appropriate. The person who lost a sense of control needs to be empowered to make this decision. In short, the person who betrayed their partner's trust often feels as if things are improving faster than the person who was betrayed.

Betrayed Partner

It may take a lot of time for you to feel safe and secure again. Forgive your partner when you no longer hold feelings of anger and resentment about what happened and when you can view how things are going in your relationship in a positive light. Don't let your desire to have things get back to normal rush the process of forgiveness. If you're holding a grudge or still feel some bitterness about what happened, honor your emotions and express them to your partner.

Four months after Brian and Ashley worked at repairing their relationship, things were good—Brian trusted Ashley and developed a greater appreciation for their relationship. Realizing that the two of them could work together, even when things seemed broken beyond repair, helped them gain a greater sense of confidence in each other. Brian saw Ashley in a new light, as someone he could build a life with no matter what came their way. His feelings about the past were just that—in the past. He decided to move back in with Ashley, and they're now enjoying the next chapter in their lives.

Maria and George are still struggling. Things have definitely improved—Maria feels less anger and resentment than she did at first, but still doesn't understand her husband's adultery. They're continuing counseling, and George is still trying to understand his feelings. At this point, they're committed to make it work, but they realize they have a long way to go.

Recovering from a betrayal and forgiveness both take time. Forgiveness comes when the person who has been harmed no longer feels the need to get even and is able to see the relationship positively.

Repairing Betrayed Partner's Trust

While you may feel that you've done everything you can to make things better, the decision on if and when you're forgiven is not up to you. You may feel that you've put in the effort and should be forgiven, but this should happen according to your partner's time frame, not yours. Don't put pressure on your partner to forgive you. Doing so can take away his or her sense of being in control. Pressuring your partner to forgive you will only stall the progress you're making. Keep honoring your commitments until your partner decides to forgive you. The process takes time, and you don't have a say in how long it's going to take.

Putting It All Together

The key to solving an intimate betrayal involves creating mutual understanding of what transpired. Both individuals have to understand and acknowledge where the other person is coming from. By understanding each other's perspectives, couples can identify concrete, verifiable steps that can be taken to resolve the breach of trust. By working together toward mutually agreed-upon goals, couples can solve problems and learn to trust each other again.

Takeaways

- The person who betrayed their partner's trust needs to explain why the betrayal occurred.
- Both parties need to create a plan of action, which addresses the problems that have been identified.
- It's important for couples to monitor their progress and explicitly talk about their successes and setbacks.
- Ultimately, the person who was betrayed gets to decide when, and if, forgiveness occurs.

CHAPTER 10

Forgiveness and Beyond

W E WROTE THIS book to help you and your partner better understand and overcome an intimate betrayal. Even if your relationship is ideal, some type of betrayal will most likely emerge. Due to the dynamics of our relationships, transgressions are part and parcel of being intimate (the Paradox of Intimacy). The real strength of a relationship is not determined by how happy you are when everything is going great, but by how well you and your partner work together when hardships threaten to tear you apart.

Forgiveness takes time and happens when you can reflect on the incident in light of the *entire* context of your relationship. In other words, an act of betrayal should not define you or your relationship. The process of forgiveness involves fully understanding the transgression, uncovering why it happened, and reflecting upon that reason, and then working toward creating a better future with your partner. Forgiveness doesn't mean you condone what happened. Rather, it involves letting go of negative feelings about what happened, not seeking revenge or holding a grudge, and viewing a partner, but not necessarily his or her betrayal, in a new and positive way.

Not being able to forgive a spouse or partner creates distance, leads to feelings of anger and isolation, and can have a negative impact on your health. In fact, without forgiveness, you can't truly reap the benefits of being in an intimate relationship. If you can't get over your anger and are still holding a grudge, or your partner continues to betray your trust with little regard for your well-being, then it's probably time to reevaluate your relationship. Relationships are supposed to add value to your life. If things are not working out, or if your partner is consistently putting his or her own needs ahead of yours, it might be time to consider other options, such as leaving.

If you *can* successfully and completely forgive, which is what we hope for you, you've not only put the incident behind you, but you've also transcended to a new place in your relationship equipped with tools to be better listeners, empathizers, and partners to one another.

We also want to leave you with some communication strategies designed to help you have a better relationship after dealing with an intimate betrayal.

Ask Questions Carefully. After recovering from a betrayal (especially if it involves infidelity), it's normal to be a little paranoid and want to ask pointed questions such as, "Where did you go after work?" "Who did you talk to?" "What did you talk about?" But doing so can work against you.

As we've explained, when people are asked direct or accusatory questions, especially related to a betrayal, they become defensive regardless if they're guilty or not. It's an unconsciously driven response to want to protect oneself. The reasoning goes like this: *My partner is asking me a bunch of direct questions. I must have done something wrong. I don't want to get in trouble. I should keep my answers short and vague.* Asking direct questions leads to short, brief answers. This, in turn, often provokes suspicion, leading to more direct questioning, and more cautious responses. This pattern of interaction can snowball and create negative feelings for everyone involved.

To protect yourself from this trap, avoid asking questions directly, but engage the topic through self-disclosure. Bring up topics by sharing your own point of view. Rather than ask, "Where were you all day?" talk about where *you* went. For example, when Brian and Ashley were trying to work through the aftermath of her affair, he often started talking about the people he ran into throughout the day, and Ashley felt comfortable sharing the same information. Brian was able to find out what she'd been doing in a natural and spontaneous way. Starting a conversation through self-disclosure helps foster intimacy and trust.

React Calmly. It's also useful to react calmly when your partner tells you something you don't want to hear. Many people, especially individuals with a concerned or cool style of attachment, react negatively when they hear unwelcome information. However, if you react in an overly upset, frantic, or hostile way when your partner is actually telling you the truth, don't be surprised when he or she starts altering the truth (lying) to make you happy. The more you punish your partner for telling the truth (even by giving him or her the cold shoulder), the less likely the truth will be told.

Remember, you're more than just your emotions—you have the ability to pause, think, and reflect before you react. Creating a safe environment for your partner to share information with you is critical to reducing future acts of betrayal.

We're not saying that you have to be happy or agree with what your partner tells you; far from it. In fact, it's important to be honest with your partner about your feelings. Real relationships require real conversations. And the style and tone you take with your partner matters a great deal. You can be upset and disagree with your partner, but do so in a calm and collected manner. Pay attention to the tone of your voice, facial expressions, and word choice, and be aware of your overt displays of anger and hostility. It's great to express yourself, but be sure to do so in a way that doesn't run roughshod over your partner.

Try to Be Empathetic. Not only should you avoid punishing your partner for telling you the truth, you should also take steps to make him or her feel understood. Even when your partner is clearly wrong, try being empathetic when conversing with him or her. You undoubtedly have a desire to feel understood; this is also what your partner *wants* from you.

Everyone, including your partner, is entitled to his or her feelings and thoughts, so it's important for you both to be able to express yourselves in your relationship. The trick is to see the issue from your partner's point of view, while also holding onto your own perspective. Essentially you have to become comfortable disagreeing with your partner while not being disagreeable. By creating an environment in which your partner feels understood, he or she will continue to share important matters with you, and vice versa. The result? Fewer secrets will be kept, and fewer betrayals will occur.

Be Open. If you want your partner to tell you the truth and treat you with respect, you have to do the same. When you're struggling with a problem (including a betrayal), or a difficult issue that might upset your partner, demonstrate your willingness to confront such issues head on. Talk to your partner about what's bothering you using the techniques for communication provided in Chapter 7. Your partner will respect you for doing so and return the favor.

Balance the Power. Power differences exist in all relationships based on the unique resources that each person brings to the table. For example, one person may make more money, while the other person is more likable, resulting in different sources of power in their relationship. If there's a conflict related to spending, the higher earner may have a larger say. But when it comes to decisions about socializing, the partner who has the more outgoing personality probably holds sway.

In general, the person with fewer resources in a relationship is the one who is more likely to engage in deception. People who feel powerless often use deception as a means of gaining back a sense of control. So, for example, if you try to control and monitor your partner's spending, he or she will probably find ways to go around your restrictions. Or if you're dictating what your partner does with his or her free time, don't be surprised when your partner is suddenly too tired to go out. No one likes to feel that their sense of power is being taken away; they're likely to find ways to fight back (even if they aren't aware they're doing it), which may result in a major transgression.

To create a better balance of power in your relationship, go out of your way to involve each other in the decision-making process. For instance, when planning family vacations, make sure that everyone has a say. A partner who doesn't feel like his or her opinion matters will likely find ways to wriggle out of agreements, be uncooperative, or even sabotage whatever plans are set. The more time you can engage in collaborative decision-making from the start, the less likely a partner will work behind the scenes to undo decisions (in other words, deceive you). Balancing power often means giving up some power. The more you share power and make each other feel included and valued, the less likely you'll encounter deception and betrayal.

Accept Your Partner. It helps to remember that no one is perfect. No matter how much you love your partner—and he or she loves you—your trust will be betrayed from time to time. We can't live up to all of the expectations that are placed on us. Indeed, we can't always live up to our own expectations, let alone someone else's.

Putting It All Together

Working with your partner in a respectful and collaborative way can put you on the path to forgiveness and rebuilding trust. Only through the process of sharing feelings, listening to each other, finding solutions, and accomplishing goals can couples overcome an intimate betrayal.

Takeaways

- Forgiveness occurs when couples are able to work together to create a stronger, more trusting relationship.
- It helps to implement communication strategies that foster more openness and sharing in your relationship.

Afterword

THROUGHOUT THIS BOOK, we have been stressing the benefits of collaboration. It's through working together as a team that couples can overcome the problems they face. This book is also a testament to collaboration: To the joint effort of hundreds of researchers who have spent their lives studying relationships and sharing their knowledge with others. To the efforts of thousands of individuals who are struggling with an intimate betrayal and reached out to us for advice and, by doing so, have helped us identify the most pressing issues people need help with. To the teamwork the two of us achieved to take Tim's research on deception and attachment and translate it into ways that can help couples recover from a breach of trust. This book is truly the product of the combined efforts of thousands of individuals.

We know how isolating it can be to go through an intimate betrayal. There are times when your partner is probably the last person you feel like talking to. And family and friends often lack the knowledge and insights needed to help you recover from a major transgression. We hope that you'll reach out to us and the community we're creating online—a community where you can engage with other readers of this book and learn from the wisdom of the crowd—www.brokentrust.com. By helping each other through difficult times, we hope to build a collaborative community that is stronger and wiser than its individual parts.

References

If you're interested in knowing more about the research underlying *Broken Trust,* you can find detailed notes highlighting the academic scholarship discussed in this book online at www.brokentrust.com/community/notes.

Afifi, W. A., & Burgoon, J. K. (1998). "We never talk about that": A comparison of cross-sex friendships and dating relationships on uncertainty and topic avoidance. *Personal Relationships, 5,* 255-272.

Afifi, W. A., Falato, W. L., & Weiner, J. L. (2001). Identity concerns following a severe relational transgression: The role of discovery method for the relational outcomes of infidelity. *Journal of Social and Personal Relationships, 18,* 291-308.

Afifi, W. A., & Metts, S. (1998). Characteristics and consequences of expectation violations in close relationships. *Journal of Social and Personal Relationships, 15,* 365-392.

Ainsworth, M. D. S., Blehar, M. S., Waters, E., & Wall, S. (1978). *Patterns of attachment: A psychological study of the strange situation.* Hillsdale, NJ: Lawrence Erlbaum.

Altman, I., & Taylor, D. A. (1973). *Social penetration: The development of interpersonal relationships.* New York: Holt, Rinehart & Winston.

Anderson, D. E., Ansfield, M. E., & DePaulo, B. M. (1999). Love's best habit: Deception in the context of relationships. In P. Philippot, R. S. Feldman, & E. J. Coats (Eds.), *The social* context of nonverbal behavior (pp. 372-409). New York: Cambridge University Press.

Arcimowicz, B., Cantarero, K., & Soroko, E. (2015). Motivation and consequences of lying. A qualitative analysis of everyday lying. In *Forum Qualitative Sozialforschung/Forum: Qualitative Social Research* (Vol. 16, No. 3).

Argyle, M., & Henderson, M. (1985). *The anatomy of relationships.* London: Methuen.

Argyle, M., Henderson, M., & Furnham, A. (1985). The rules of social relationships. *British Journal of Social Psychology*, 24(2), 125-139.

Arkes, H. R., & Blumer, C. (1985). The psychology of sunk cost. *Organizational Behavior and Human Decision Processes*, 35(1), 124-140.

Aron, A., Norman, C. C., Aron, E. N., McKenna, C., & Heyman, R. E. (2000). Couples' shared participation in novel and arousing activities and experienced relationship quality. *Journal of Personality and Social Psychology*, 78(2), 273-284.

Back, M. D., Schmukle, S. C., & Egloff, B. (2010). Why are narcissists so charming at first sight? Decoding the narcissism–popularity link at zero acquaintance. *Journal of Personality and Social Psychology*, 98(1), 132-145.

Baldwin, M. W., Fehr, B., Keedian, E., Seidel, M., & Thomson, D. W. (1993). An exploration of the relational schemata underlying attachment styles: Self-report and lexical decision approaches. *Personality and Social Psychology Bulletin*, 19, 746-754.

Bartholomew, K. (1990). Avoidance of intimacy: An attachment perspective. *Journal of Social and Personal Relationships*, 7, 147-178.

Bartholomew, K., & Horowitz, L. M. (1991). Attachment styles among young adults: a test of a four-category model. *Journal of Personality and Social Psychology*, 61(2), 226-244.

Baumeister, R. F., Heatherton, T. F., & Tice, D. M. (1994). *Losing control: How and why people fail at self-regulation.* San Diego: Academic Press.

Baumeister, R. F., & Leary, M.R. (1995). The need to belong: Desire for interpersonal attachments as a fundamental human motivation. *Psychological Bulletin*, 117, 497-529.

Baxter, L. A. (1984). Trajectories of relationship disengagement. *Journal of Social and Personal Relationships*, 1(1), 29-48.

Baxter, L. A. (1986). Gender differences in the hetero-sexual relationship rules embedded in break-up accounts. *Journal of Social and Personal Relationships*, 3(3), 289-306.

Baxter, L. A. (1990). Dialectical contractions in relational development. *Journal of Social and Personal Relationships*, 7, 69-88.

Baxter, L. A., & Montgomery, B. M. (1996). *Relating: Dialogues and dialectics*. New York: Guilford Press.

Baxter, L. A., & Wilmot, W. W. (1985). Taboo topics in close relationships. *Journal of Social and Personal Relationships*, 2(3), 253-269.

Beaulieu-Pelletier, G., Philippe, F. L., Lecours, S., & Couture, S. (2011). The role of attachment avoidance in extradyadic sex. *Attachment & Human Development*, 13(3), 293-313.

Berkman, L. F., & Syme, S. L. (1979). Social networks, host resistance, and mortality: A nine-year follow-up study of Alameda County residents. *American Journal of Epidemiology*, 103, 186-204.

Berlin, L. J., Cassidy, J., & Appleyard, K. (2008). The influence of early attachments on other relationships. In J. Cassidy and P. R. Shaver (Eds.), *Handbook of attachment: Theory, research and clinical applications* (pp. 333-347). New York: Guilford Press.

Bernstein, R. E., Laurent, S. M., Nelson, B. W., & Laurent, H. K. (2015). Perspective-taking induction mitigates the effect of partner attachment avoidance on self–partner overlap. *Personal Relationships*, 22, 356-367.

Berscheid, E. (1985). Compatibility, interdependence, and emotion. In W. Ickes (Ed.), *Compatible and incompatible relationships* (pp. 143-161). New York: Springer.

Birnie, C., McClure, M. J., Lydon, J. E., & Holmberg, D. (2009). Attachment avoidance and commitment aversion: A script for relationship failure. *Personal Relationships*, 16(1), 79-97.

Bochner, A. P. (1982). On the efficacy of openness in close relationships. In M. Burgoon (Ed.), *Communication yearbook 5* (pp. 109-124). New Brunswick: Transaction Books.

Boon, S. D. (1994). Dispelling doubt and uncertainty: Trust in romantic relationships. In S. Duck (Ed.), *Dynamics of relationships: Understanding relationship processes* (pp. 86-111). Thousand Oaks: SAGE Publications.

Boon, S. D., & Sulsky, L. M. (1997). Attributions of blame and forgiveness in romantic relationships: A policy-capturing study. *Journal of Social Behavior & Personality, 12,* 19-44.

Bowlby, J. (1969). *Attachment and loss. Vol 1. Attachment.* New York: Basic Books.

Bowlby, J. (1973). *Attachment and loss. Vol 2. Separation: Anxiety and anger.* New York: Basic Books.

Bowlby, J. (1980). *Attachment and loss. Vol 3. Loss: Sadness and depression.* New York: Basic Books.

Bowman, M. L. (1990). Coping efforts and marital satisfaction: Measuring marital coping and its correlates. *Journal of Marriage and the Family, 52,* 463-474.

Brehm, J. W. (1966). *A theory of psychological reactance.* New York: Academic Press.

Brennan, K. A., Clark, C. L., & Shaver, P. R. (1998). Self-report measurement of adult attachment: An integrative overview. In J. A. Simpson & W. S. Rholes (Eds.), *Attachment theory and close relationships* (pp. 46-76). New York: Guilford Press.

Brumbaugh, C. C., Baren, A., & Agishtein, P. (2014). Attraction to attachment insecurity: Flattery, appearance, and status's role in mate preferences. *Personal Relationships, 21*(2), 288-308.

Brumbaugh, C. C., & Fraley, R. C. (2010). Adult attachment and dating strategies: How do insecure people attract mates? *Personal Relationships, 17*(4), 599-614.

Buller, D. B., & Burgoon, J. K. (1998). Emotional expression in the deception process. In P. A. Anderson and L. K. Guerrero (Eds.), *Handbook of communication and emotion* (pp. 381-402). San Diego: Academic Press.

Burleson, B. R. (2003). Emotional support skills. In J. O. Greene and B. R. Burleson (Eds.), *Handbook of communication and social interaction skills* (pp. 551-594). Mahwah, NJ: Lawrence Erlbaum Associates Publishers.

Burleson, B. R., Albrecht, T. L., & Sarason, I. G. (1994). *Communication of social support: Messages, interactions, relationships, and community.* Thousand Oaks: SAGE Publications.

Butler, E. A., & Gross, J. J. (2004). Hiding feelings in social contexts: Out of sight is not out of mind. In P. Philippot and R.

S. Feldman (Eds.), *The regulation of emotion* (pp. 101-126). Mahwah, NJ: Lawrence Erlbaum Associates.

Camden, C., Motley, M., T., & Wilson, A. (1984). White lies in interpersonal communication: A taxonomy and preliminary investigation of social motivations. *The Western Journal of Speech Communication, 48*, 309-325.

Campbell, W. K., Foster, C. A., & Finkel, E. J. (2002). Does self-love lead to love for others? A story of narcissistic game playing. *Journal of Personality and Social Psychology, 83*(2), 340-354.

Canary, D. J., Stafford, L., Hause, K. S., & Wallace, L. A. (1993). An inductive analysis of relational maintenance strategies: Comparisons among lovers, relatives, friends, and others. *Communication Research Reports, 10*(1), 3-14.

Carothers, B. J., & Reis, H. T. (2013). Men and women are from earth: Examining the latent structure of gender. *Journal of Personality and Social Psychology, 104*, 385-407.

Carson, J. W., Carson, K. M., Gil, K. M., & Baucom, D. H. (2007). Self-expansion as a mediator of relationship improvements in a mindfulness intervention. *Journal of Marital and Family Therapy, 33*(4), 517-528.

Chbosky, S. (2012). *The perks of being a wallflower.* New York: Simon and Schuster.

Christensen, A. (1988). Dysfunctional interaction patterns in couples. In P. Noller & M. E. Fitzpatrick (Eds.), *Perspectives on marital interaction* (Vol. 1, pp. 31-52). Clevedon, England: Multilingual Matters.

Clark, M. S., & Mills, J. R. (2011). A theory of communal (and exchange) relationships. In P. A. Van Lange, A. W. Kruglanski, and E. T. Higgins (Eds). *Handbook of theories of social psychology: Volume two* (pp. 232-250). Thousand Oaks: SAGE Publications.

Clark, M. S., Pataki, S. P., & Carver, V. H. (1996). Some thoughts and findings on self-presentation of emotions in relationships. In G. J. O. Fletcher & J. Fitness (Eds.), *Knowledge structures in close relationships: A social psychological approach,* (pp. 247-274). Mahwah, NJ: Lawrence Erlbaum Associates.

Cloven, D. H., & Roloff, M. E. (1993). The chilling effect of aggressive potential on the expression of complaints in intimate relationships. *Communication Monographs, 60*, 199-219.

Cody, M. J., Kersten, L., Braaten, D. O., & Dickson, R. (1992). Coping with relational dissolutions: Attributions, account credibility, and plans for resolving conflicts. In J. H. Harvey, T. Orbuch, & A. Weber (Eds.), *Attributions, accounts, and close relationships* (pp. 93-115). New York: Springer US.

Cole, T. (2001). Lying to the one you love: The use of deception in romantic relationships. *Journal of Social and Personal Relationships, 18,* 107-129.

Cole, T. (2006). Intimacy, deception, truth and lies: The paradox of being close. *Entelechy: Mind and culture, 7.*

Cole, T. (2014). Betrayal. In T. R. Levine (Ed.) *Encyclopedia of Deception* (pp. 72-74). Thousand Oaks: SAGE Publications.

Cole, T. & Leets, L. (1999). Attachment styles and intimate television viewing: Insecurely forming relationships in a parasocial way. *Journal of Social and Personal Relationships, 16*(4), 495-511.

Cole, T., & Teboul, JC. B. (2004). Non-zero sum collaboration, reciprocity and the preference for similarity: Developing an adaptive model of close relational functioning. *Personal Relationships, 11,* 135-160.

Collins, N. L., & Read, S. J. (1990). Adult attachment, working models, and relationship quality in dating couples. *Journal of Personality and Social Psychology, 58*(4), 644-663.

Cupach, W. R., Canary, D. J., & Spitzberg, B. H. (2010). *Competence in interpersonal conflict* (Second Edition). Long Grove, IL: Waveland Press.

Cupach, W. R., & Metts, S. (1994). *Facework.* Thousand Oaks: SAGE Publications.

Dainton, M. (2007). Attachment and marital maintenance. *Communication Quarterly, 55*(3), 283-298.

Darby, B. W., & Schlenker, B. R. (1982). Children's reactions to apologies. *Journal of Personality and Social Psychology, 43*(4), 742-753.

Davis, J. R., & Gold, G. J. (2011). An examination of emotional empathy, attributions of stability, and the link between perceived remorse and forgiveness. *Personality and Individual Differences, 50*(3), 392-397.

Demo, D. H., & Ganong, L. H. (1994). *Divorce. Families and change: Coping with stressful events.* Thousand Oaks: SAGE Publications.

DePaulo, B. M., Charlton, K., Cooper, H., Lindsay, J. J., & Muhlenbruck, L. (1997). The accuracy-confidence correlation in the detection of deception. *Personality and Social Psychology Review,* 1, 346-357.

DePaulo, B. M., Kashy, D. A., Kirkendol, S. E., Wyer, M. M., & Epstein, J. A. (1996). Lying in everyday life. *Journal of Personality and Social Psychology,* 70, 979-995.

Derlega, V. J., Metts, S., Petronio, S., & Margulis, S. T. (1993). *Self-disclosure.* Thousand Oaks: SAGE Publications.

DeWall, C. N., Lambert, N. M., Slotter, E. B., Pond Jr, R. S., Deckman, T., Finkel, E. J., Luchies, L. B., & Fincham, F. D. (2011). So far away from one's partner, yet so close to romantic alternatives: Avoidant attachment, interest in alternatives, and infidelity. *Journal of Personality and Social Psychology,* 101(6), 1302-1316.

Domingue, R., & Mollen, D. (2009). Attachment and conflict communication in adult romantic relationships. *Journal of Social and Personal Relationships,* 26(5), 678-696.

Dufner, M., Rauthmann, J. F., Czarna, A. Z., & Denissen, J. J. (2013). Are narcissists sexy? Zeroing in on the effect of narcissism on short-term mate appeal. *Personality and Social Psychology Bulletin,* 39(7), 870-882.

Dutton, D. G., Saunders, K., Starzomski, A., & Bartholomew, K. (1994). Intimacy-anger and insecure attachment as precursors of abuse in intimate relationships. *Journal of Applied Social Psychology,* 24, 1367-1386.

Eidelson, R. J., & Epstein, N. (1982). Cognition and relationship maladjustment: Development of a measure of dysfunctional relationship beliefs. *Journal of Consulting and Clinical Psychology,* 50(5), 715-720.

Eisenberger, N. I., Lieberman, M. D., & Williams, K. D. (2003). Does rejection hurt? An fMRI study of social exclusion. *Science,* 302(5643), 290-292.

Ekman, P. (1985). *Telling lies.* New York: W. W. Norton.

Emmers, T. M., & Canary, D. J. (1996). The effect of uncertainty reducing strategies on young couples' relational repair and intimacy. *Communication Quarterly*, 44(2), 166-182.

Ennis, E., Vrij, A., & Chance, C. (2008). Individual differences and lying in everyday life. *Journal of Social and Personal Relationships*, 25(1), 105-118.

Feeney, B. C., & Collins, N. L. (2015). Thriving through relationships. *Current Opinion in Psychology*, 1, 22-28.

Feeney, J. A. (2005). Hurt feelings in couple relationships: Exploring the role of attachment and perceptions of personal injury. *Personal Relationships*, 12(2), 253-271.

Feeney, J. A. (2008). Adult romantic attachment: Developments in the study of couple relationships. In J. Cassidy & P. R. Shaver (Eds.), *Handbook of attachment: Theory, research and clinical applications* (pp. 456-481). New York: Guilford Press.

Feeney, J. A., & Noller, P. (1990). Attachment style as a predictor of adult romantic relationships. *Journal of Personality and Social Psychology*, 58(2), 281-291.

Feeney, J. A., & Noller, P. (1992). Attachment style and romantic love: Relationship dissolution. *Australian Journal of Psychology*, 44(2), 69-74.

Fiedler, K., & Walka, I. (1993). Training lie detectors to use nonverbal cues instead of global heuristics. *Human Communication Research*, 20, 199-223.

Fincham, F. D., & Beach, S. R. (2002). Forgiveness in marriage: Implications for psychological aggression and constructive communication. *Personal Relationships*, 9, 239-251.

Fincham, F. D. & Beach, S. R. (2013). Gratitude and forgiveness in relationships. In J. A. Simpson & L. Campbell (Eds.), *Oxford handbook of close relationships* (pp. 638-663). New York: Oxford University Press.

Fincham, F. D., Beach, S. R., & Davila, J. (2007). Longitudinal relations between forgiveness and conflict resolution in marriage. *Journal of Family Psychology*, 21, 542-545.

Fincham, F. D., Hall, J. H., & Beach, S. R. (2005). Til lack of forgiveness doth us part: Forgiveness in marriage. In Worthington Jr, E. L. (Ed.), *Handbook of forgiveness* (pp. 207-226). New York: Routledge.

Fincham, F. D., Jackson, H., & Beach, S. R. (2005). Transgression severity and forgiveness: Different moderators for objective and subjective severity. *Journal of Social and Clinical Psychology*, 24, 860-875.

Fincham, F. D., Paleari, F., & Regalia, C. (2002). Forgiveness in marriage: The role of relationship quality, attributions, and empathy. *Personal Relationships*, 9, 27-37.

Finkel, E. J., Hui, C. M., Carswell, K. L., & Larson, G. M. (2014). The suffocation of marriage: Climbing Mount Maslow without enough oxygen. *Psychological Inquiry*, 25(1), 1-41.

Finkel, E. J., Slotter, E. B., Luchies, L. B., Walton, G. M., & Gross, J. J. (2013). A brief intervention to promote conflict reappraisal preserves marital quality over time. *Psychological Science*, 24, 1595-1601.

Finkenauer, C., & Hazam, H. (2000). Disclosure and secrecy in marriage: Do both contribute to marital satisfaction? *Journal of Social and Personal Relationships*, 17, 245-263.

Fischer, A. H., Manstead, A. S., Evers, C., Timmers, M., & Valk, G. (2004). Motives and norms underlying emotion regulation. In P. Philippot & R. S. Feldman (Eds.). *The regulation of emotion* (187-210). Hove, United Kingdom: Psychology Press.

Fish, J. N., Pavkov, T. W., Wetchler, J. L., & Bercik, J. (2012). Characteristics of those who participate in infidelity: The role of adult attachment and differentiation in extradyadic experiences. *American Journal of Family Therapy*, 40(3), 214-229.

Fisher, H. (2004). *Why we love: The nature and chemistry of romantic love*. New York: Henry Holt and Company.

Fitness, J. (2001). Betrayal, rejection, revenge, and forgiveness: An interpersonal script approach. In M. Leary (Ed.) *Interpersonal rejection* (pp. 73-103). New York: Oxford University Press.

Fitness, J., & Fletcher, G. J. (1993). Love, hate, anger, and jealousy in close relationships: A prototype and cognitive appraisal analysis. *Journal of Personality and Social Psychology*, 65(5), 942-958.

Fitzpatrick, M. A. (1988). *Between husbands and wives: Communication in marriage*. Newbury Park, CA: SAGE.

Fraley, R. C., Roisman, G. I., Booth-LaForce, C., Owen, M. T., & Holland, A. S. (2013). Interpersonal and genetic origins of adult attachment styles: A longitudinal study from infancy to early adulthood. *Journal of Personality and Social Psychology*, 104(5), 817-857.

Fredrickson, B. L. (1998). What good are positive emotions? *Review of General Psychology*, 2(3), 300-319.

Frost, D. M., & Forrester, C. (2013). Closeness discrepancies in romantic relationships implications for relational well-being, stability, and mental health. *Personality and Social Psychology Bulletin*, 39, 456-469.

Furnham, A., Richards, S. C., & Paulhus, D. L. (2013). The dark triad of personality: A 10 year review. *Social and Personality Psychology Compass*, 7(3), 199-216.

Galliher, R. V., Rostosky, S. S., Welsh, D. P., & Kawaguchi, M. C. (1999). Power and psychological well-being in late adolescent romantic relationships. *Sex Roles*, 40(9-10), 689-710.

Gibb, J. (1961). Defensive communication. *Journal of Communication*, 11, 141-148.

Gilbert, D. T., Krull, D. S., & Malone, P. S. (1990). Unbelieving the unbelievable: Some problems in the rejection of false information. *Journal of Personality and Social Psychology*, 59(4), 601-613.

Gillath, O., Sesko, A. K., Shaver, P. R., & Chun, D. S. (2010). Attachment, authenticity, and honesty: Dispositional and experimentally induced security can reduce self-and other-deception. *Journal of Personality and Social Psychology*, 98(5), 841-855.

Girme, Y. U., Overall, N. C., & Faingataa, S. (2014). "Date nights" take two: The maintenance function of shared relationship activities. *Personal Relationships*, 21(1), 125-149.

Givertz, M., Woszidlo, A., Segrin, C., & Knutson, K. (2013). Direct and indirect effects of attachment orientation on relationship quality and loneliness in married couples. *Journal of Social and Personal Relationships*, 30(8), 1096-1120.

Glass, S. P., & Staeheli, J. C. (2003). *Not" just friends": Protect your relationship from infidelity and heal the trauma of betrayal*. New York: Free Press.

Goodwin, R., & Gaines, S. O. (2004). Relationships beliefs and relationship quality across cultures: Country as a moderator of dysfunctional beliefs and relationship quality in three former Communist societies. *Personal Relationships*, 11(3), 267-279.

Gordon, A. M., & Chen, S. (2015). Do you get where I'm coming from? Perceived understanding buffers against the negative impact of conflict on relationship satisfaction. *Journal of Personality and Social Psychology*, 110(2), 239-260.

Gordon, K. C., Baucom, D. H., & Snyder, D. K. (2005). Forgiveness in couples: Divorce, infidelity, and couples therapy. In E. L. Worthington Jr, (Ed.), *Handbook of forgiveness* (pp. 407-421). New York: Routledge.

Gottman, J. M. (1994). *What predicts divorce? The relationship between marital processes and marital outcomes.* Hillsdale, NJ: Lawrence Erlbaum Associates.

Gottman, J. M., & Levenson, R. W. (1992). Marital processes predictive of later dissolution: Behavior, physiology, and health. *Journal of Personality and Social Psychology*, 63(2), 221-233.

Guerrero, L. K. (1998). Attachment-style differences in the experience and expression of romantic jealousy. *Personal Relationships*, 5(3), 273-291.

Gunderson, P. R., & Ferrari, J. R. (2008). Forgiveness of sexual cheating in romantic relationships: Effects of discovery method, frequency of offense, and presence of apology. *North American Journal of Psychology*, 10(1), 1-14.

Guthrie, J., & Kunkel, A. (2013). Tell me sweet (and not-so-sweet) little lies: Deception in romantic relationships. *Communication Studies*, 64(2), 141-157.

Hadden, B. W., Smith, C. V., & Webster, G. D. (2014). Relationship duration moderates associations between attachment and relationship quality meta-analytic support for the temporal adult romantic attachment model. *Personality and Social Psychology Review*, 18(1), 42-58.

Hample, D. (1980). Purposes and effects of lying. *Southern Speech Communication Journal*, 46, 33-47.

Hansson, R. O., Jones, W. H., & Fletcher, W. L. (1990). Troubled relationships in later life: Implications for support. *Journal of Social and Personal Relationships*, 7(4), 451-463.

Hare, R. D. (1991). *The Hare psychopathy checklist-revised: Manual.* Multi-Health Systems, Incorporated.

Harms, P. D. (2011). Adult attachment styles in the workplace. *Human Resource Management Review*, 21(4), 285-296.

Harris, S. (2014). *Waking up: A guide to spirituality without religion.* New York: Simon and Schuster.

Harvey, J. H. & Omarzu, J. (1997). Minding the close relationship. *Personality and Social Psychology Review*, 1, 224-240.

Hatfield, E. (1984). The dangers of intimacy. In V. J. Derlega (Ed.), *Communication, intimacy, and close relationships*, (pp. 207-220). New York: Academic Press.

Hawkins, D. N., & Booth, A. (2005). Unhappily ever after: Effects of long-term, low-quality marriages on well-being. *Social Forces*, 84(1), 451-471.

Hazan, C., & Shaver, P. (1987). Romantic love conceptualized as an attachment process. *Journal of Personality and Social Psychology*, 52(3), 511-524.

Heffernan, M. E., Fraley, R. C., Vicary, A. M., & Brumbaugh, C. C. (2012). Attachment features and functions in adult romantic relationships. *Journal of Social and Personal Relationships*, 29, 671-693.

Hill, E. M., Young, J. P., & Nord, J. L. (1994). Childhood adversity, attachment security, and adult relationships: A preliminary study. *Ethology and Sociobiology*, 15(5), 323-338.

Hindy, C. G., & Schwarz, J. C. (1994). Anxious romantic attachment in adult relationships. In M. B. Sperling & W. H. Berman (Eds.) *Attachment in adults: Clinical and developmental perspectives* (pp. 179-203). New York: Guilford Press.

Holmes, B. M., & Johnson, K. R. (2009). Adult attachment and romantic partner preference: A review. *Journal of Social and Personal Relationships*, 26, 833-852.

Holmes, J. G. (1991). Trust and the appraisal process in close relationships. In W. H. Jones & D. Perlman (Eds.), *Advances in personal relationships: A research annual (Vol. 2)* (pp. 57-104). London: Jessica Kingsley Publishers.

Holmes, J. G., & Rempel, J. K. (1989). Trust in close relationships. In C. Hendrick (Ed.), *Close relationships. Review of personality and social psychology* (Vol. 10, pp. 187-220). Thousand Oaks: SAGE Publications.

Holt-Lunstad, J., Smith, T. B., & Layton, J. B. (2010). Social relationships and mortality risk: A meta-analytic review. *PLoS Medicine*, 7, (7).

Ickes, W., & Simpson, J. A. (2001). Motivational aspects of empathic accuracy. In G. J. O. Fletcher & M. Clark (Eds.), *Blackwell handbook of social psychology: Interpersonal processes* (pp. 218-249). Oxford: Blackwell.

Impett, E. A., & Gordon, A. M. (2010). Why do people sacrifice to approach rewards versus to avoid costs? Insights from attachment theory. *Personal Relationships*, 17, 299-315.

Jakobwitz, S., & Egan, V. (2006). The dark triad and normal personality traits. *Personality and Individual Differences*, 40(2), 331-339.

Jang, S. A., Smith, S., & Levine, T. (2002). To stay or to leave? The role of attachment styles in communication patterns and potential termination of romantic relationships following discovery of deception. *Communication Monographs*, 69, 236-252.

Jonason, P. K., Li, N. P., Webster, G. D., & Schmitt, D. P. (2009). The dark triad: Facilitating a short-term mating strategy in men. *European Journal of Personality*, 23(1), 5-18.

Jonason, P. K., & Webster, G. D. (2010). The dirty dozen: A concise measure of the dark triad. *Psychological Assessment*, 22(2), 420-432.

Jones, E., & Gallois, C. (1989). Spouses' impressions of rules for communication in public and private marital conflicts. *Journal of Marriage and the Family*, 51, 957-967.

Jones, W. H., & Burdette, M. P. (1994). Betrayal in relationships. In A. L Weber & J. H. Harvey (Eds.), *Perspectives on close relationships* (pp. 243-262). Needham Heights, MA: Allyn and Bacon.

Jones, W. H., Couch, L., & Scott, S. (1997). Trust and betrayal: The psychology of getting along and getting ahead. In R. Hogan, J. Johnson & S. Briggs (Eds.), *Handbook of personality psychology* (pp. 465-482). New York: Academic Press.

Kachadourian, L. K., Fincham, F., & Davila, J. (2004). The tendency to forgive in dating and married couples: The role of attachment and relationship satisfaction. *Personal Relationships*, 11, 373-393.

Kane, H. S., Jaremka, L. M., Guichard, A. C., Ford, M. B., Collins, N. L., & Feeney, B. C. (2007). Feeling supported and feeling satisfied: How one partner's attachment style predicts the other partner's relationship experiences. *Journal of Social and Personal Relationships*, 24, 535-555.

Kelley, D. (1998). The communication of forgiveness. *Communication Studies*, 49, 255-271.

Kelley, H. H., & Thibaut, J. W. (1978). *Interpersonal relations: A theory of interdependence*. New York: John Wiley and Sons.

Kelly, A. E., & McKillop, K. J. (1996). Consequences of revealing personal secrets. *Psychological Bulletin*, 120, 450-465.

Kirkpatrick, L. A., & Davis, K. E. (1994). Attachment style, gender, and relationship stability: A longitudinal analysis. *Journal of Personality and Social Psychology*, 66, 502-512.

Kline, S. L., & Stafford, L. (2004). A comparison of interaction rules and interaction frequency in relationship to marital quality. *Communication Reports*, 17, 11-26.

Knobloch, L. D. & Metts, S. (2013). Emotion in relationships. In J. A. Simpson & L. Campbell (Eds.), *Oxford handbook of close relationships* (pp. 514-534). New York: Oxford University Press.

Knobloch, L. K., & Solomon, D. H. (1999). Measuring the sources and content of relational uncertainty. *Communication Studies*, 50(4), 261-278.

Knobloch, L. K., & Solomon, D. H. (2005). Relational uncertainty and relational information processing questions without answers. *Communication Research*, 32(3), 349-388.

Kobak, R., & Madsen, S. (2008). Disruptions in attachment bonds: Implications for theory, research, and clinical intervention. In J. Cassidy & P. R. Shaver (Eds.), *Handbook of attachment: Theory, research and clinical applications* (pp. 23-47). New York: Guilford Press.

Kobak, R. R., & Sceery, A. (1988). Attachment in late adolescence: Working models, affect regulation, and representations of self and others. *Child Development*, 59, 135-146.

Koenig Kellas, J., Willer, E. K., & Trees, A. R. (2013). Communicated perspective-taking during stories of marital stress:

Spouses' perceptions of one another's perspective-taking behaviors. *Southern Communication Journal*, 78(4), 326-351.

Kok, B. E., Coffey, K. A., Cohn, A. C., Catalino, L. I., Vacharkulksemsuk, T., Aloe, S. B., Brantley, M., & Fredrickson, B. L. (2013). How positive emotions build physical health perceived positive social connections account for the upward spiral between positive emotions and vagal tone. *Psychological Science*, 24(7), 1123-1132.

Krebs, D. L., & Denton, K. (1997). Social illusions and self-deception: The evolution of biases in person perception. In J. A. Simpson & D. T. Kenrick (Eds.), *Evolutionary social psychology* (pp. 21-47). Mahwah, NJ: Lawrence Erlbaum Associates.

Kurtz, L. E., & Algoe, S. B. (2015). Putting laughter in context: Shared laughter as behavioral indicator of relationship well-being. *Personal Relationships*, 22(4), 573-590.

Larzelere, R. E., & Huston, T. L. (1980). The dyadic trust scale: Toward understanding interpersonal trust in close relationships. *Journal of Marriage and the Family*, 42, 595-604.

Leary, M. R., & Springer, C. (2001). Hurt feelings: The neglected emotion. In R. M. Kowalski (Ed.), *Aversive behaviors and relational transgressions* (pp. 151-175). Washington, DC: American Psychological Association.

Levine, T. R. (2014). Truth-Default Theory (TDT): A theory of human deception and deception detection. *Journal of Language and Social Psychology*, 33(4), 378-392

Levine, T. R., & McCornack, S. A. (1992). Linking love and lies: A formal test of the McCornack and Parks model of deception detection. *Journal of Social and Personal Relationships, 9*, 143-154.

Levitt, M. J., Silver, M. E., & Franco, N. (1996). Troublesome relationships: A part of human experience. *Journal of Social and Personal Relationships*, 13(4), 523-536.

Levy, M. B., & Davis, K. E. (1988). Lovestyles and attachment styles compared: Their relations to each other and to various relationship characteristics. *Journal of Social and Personal Relationships*, 5(4), 439-471.

Levy, T. M., & Orlans, M. (1998). *Attachment, Trauma, and Healing: Understanding and Treating Attachment Disorder in Chil-*

dren and Families. Child Welfare League of America, c/o PMDS, 9050 Junction Drive, PO Box 2019, Annapolis Junction, MD 20701-2019.

Lewis, M. (1993). The development of deception. In C. Saarni & M. Lewis (Eds.), *Lying and deception in everyday life* (pp. 90-105). New York: Guilford Press.

Lippard, P. V. (1988). "Ask me no questions, I'll tell you no lies": Situational exigencies for interpersonal deception. *Western Journal of Speech Communication, 52,* 91-103.

Livingstone, D. S. (2004). *Why we lie: The evolutionary roots of deception and the unconscious mind.* New York: St. Martin's Press.

Long, E. C., Angera, J. J., Carter, S. J., Nakamoto, M., & Kalso, M. (1999). Understanding the one you love: A longitudinal assessment of an empathy training program for couples in romantic relationships. *Family Relations, 48,* 235-242.

Marshall, T. C., Bejanyan, K., Di Castro, G., & Lee, R. A. (2013). Attachment styles as predictors of Facebook-related jealousy and surveillance in romantic relationships. *Personal Relationships, 20*(1), 1-22.

Marvin, R. S., & Britner, P. A. (2008). Normative development: The ontogeny of attachment. In J. Cassidy & P. R. Shaver (Eds.), *Handbook of attachment: Theory, research and clinical applications* (pp. 269-295). New York: Guilford Press.

Mattingly, B. A., Lewandowski, G. W., & McIntyre, K. P. (2014). "You make me a better/worse person": A two-dimensional model of relationship self-change. *Personal Relationships, 21*(1), 176-190.

McCornack, S. A. (1997). The generation of deceptive messages: Laying the groundwork for a viable theory of interpersonal deception. In J. O. Greene (Ed.), *Message production* (pp. 91-126). Hillsdale, NJ: Lawrence Erlbaum Associates.

McCornack, S. A., & Levine, T. R. (1990). When lies are uncovered: Emotional and relational outcomes of discovered deception. *Communication Monographs, 57,* 119-138.

McCornack, S. A., & Parks, M. R. (1986). Deception detection and relationship development: The other side of truth. In M. L. McLaughlin (Ed.), *Communication yearbook* 9 (pp. 377-389). Beverly Hills: SAGE Publications.

McCullough, M. E., Emmons, R. A., Kilpatrick, S. D., & Mooney, C. N. (2003). Narcissists as "victims": The role of narcissism in the perception of transgressions. *Personality and Social Psychology Bulletin*, 29, 885-893.

McCullough, M. E., Rachal, K. C., Sandage, S. J., Worthington Jr, E. L., Brown, S. W., & Hight, T. L. (1998). Interpersonal forgiving in close relationships: II. Theoretical elaboration and measurement. *Journal of Personality and Social Psychology*, 75, 1586-1603.

McCullough, M. E., Root, L. M., & Cohen, A. D. (2006). Writing about the benefits of an interpersonal transgression facilitates forgiveness. *Journal of Consulting and Clinical Psychology*, 74, 887-897.

McCullough, M. E., Worthington Jr, E. L., & Rachal, K. C. (1997). Interpersonal forgiving in close relationships. *Journal of Personality and Social Psychology*, 73, 321-336.

Menaghan, E. (1982). Measuring coping effectiveness: A panel analysis of marital problems and coping efforts. *Journal of Health and Social Behavior*, 23, 220-234.

Merrill, A. F., & Afifi, T. D. (2015). Attachment related differences in secrecy and rumination in romantic relationships. *Personal Relationships*, 22(2), 259-274.

Metts, S. (1989). An exploratory investigation of deception in close relationships. *Journal of Social and Personal Relationships*, 6, 159-179.

Metts, S. (1994). Relational transgressions. In W. R. Cupach & B. H. Spitzberg (Eds.), *The dark side of interpersonal communication* (pp. 217-239). Hillsdale, NJ: Lawrence Erlbaum Associates.

Mikulincer, M., & Shaver, P. R. (2005). Attachment theory and emotions in close relationships: Exploring the attachment-related dynamics of emotional reactions to relational events. *Personal Relationships*, 12, 149-168.

Mikulincer, M., & Shaver, P. R. (2007). *Attachment in adulthood: Structure, dynamics, and change.* New York: Guilford Press.

Mikulincer, M. & Shaver, P. R. (2008). Adult attachment and affect regulation. In J. Cassidy & P. R. Shaver (Eds.), *Handbook of attachment: Theory, research and clinical applications* (pp. 503-531). New York: Guilford Press.

Millar, K. U., & Tesser, A. (1988). Deceptive behavior in social relationships: A consequence of violated expectations. *Journal of Psychology*, 122, 263-273.

Miller, G. R., & Stiff, J. B. (1993). *Deceptive communication*. Thousand Oaks: SAGE Publications.

Miller, R. S. (1997). We always hurt the ones we love. In R. M. (Ed.), *Aversive interpersonal behaviors* (pp. 11-29). New York: Plenum Press.

Miller, R. S. (2015). *Intimate relationships* (International Edition). New York: McGraw-Hill.

Morse, C. R., & Metts, S. (2011). Situational and communicative predictors of forgiveness following a relational transgression. *Western Journal of Communication*, 75, 239-258.

Mueller, P. A., & Oppenheimer, D. M. (2014). The pen is mightier than the keyboard advantages of longhand over laptop note taking. *Psychological Science*, 25, 1159-1168.

Murray, S. L. (2005). Regulating the risks of closeness: A relationship-specific sense of felt security. *Current Directions in Psychological Science*, 14, 74-78.

Murray, S. L., & Holmes, J. G. (1997). A leap of faith? Positive illusions in romantic relationships. *Personality and Social Psychology Bulletin*, 23, 586-604.

Murray, S. L., Holmes, J. G., Bellavia, G., Griffin, D. W., & Dolderman, D. (2002). Kindred spirits? The benefits of egocentrism in close relationships. *Journal of Personality and Social Psychology*, 82, 563-581.

Murray, S. L., Holmes, J. G., Griffin, D. W., Bellavia, G., & Rose, P. (2001). The mismeasure of love: How self-doubt contaminates relationship beliefs. *Personality and Social Psychology Bulletin*, 27, 423-436.

Nathanson, A. I. (2003). Rethinking empathy. In J. Bryant, D. Roskos-Ewoldsen, & J. Cantor (Eds.), *Communication and emotion. Essays in honor of Dolf Zillmann*, (pp. 107-130). Mahwah, NJ: Lawrence Erlbaum Associates.

Newell, S. E., & Stutman, R. K. (1988). The social confrontation episode. *Communications Monographs*, 55(3), 266-285.

Ng, S. H., & Bradac, J. J. (1993). *Power in language: Verbal communication and social influence*. Thousand Oaks: SAGE Publications.

Noller, P. (1996). What is this thing called love? Defining the love that supports marriage and family. *Personal Relationships*, 3(1), 97-115.

North, J. (1987). Wrongdoing and forgiveness. *Philosophy*, 62, 499-508.

O'Leary, K. D., Acevedo, B. P., Aron, A., Huddy, L., & Mashek, D. (2012). Is long-term love more than a rare phenomenon? If so, what are its correlates? *Social Psychological and Personality Science*, 3(2), 241-249.

Ogden, C. K., Richards, I. A., Malinowski, B., & Crookshank, F. G. (1923). *The meaning of meaning* (pp. 9-12). London: Kegan Paul.

Ohbuchi, K. I., Kameda, M., & Agarie, N. (1989). Apology as aggression control: Its role in mediating appraisal of and response to harm. *Journal of Personality and Social Psychology*, 56(2), 219-227.

Oldmeadow, J. A., Quinn, S., & Kowert, R. (2013). Attachment style, social skills, and Facebook use amongst adults. *Computers in Human Behavior*, 29(3), 1142-1149.

Park, H. S., Levine, T., McCornack, S., Morrison, K., & Ferrara, M. (2002). How people really detect lies. *Communication Monographs*, 69(2), 144-157.

Parks, R. P. (1982). Ideology in interpersonal communication: Off the couch and into the world. In M. Burgoon (Ed.), *Communication yearbook* 5 (pp. 79-107). New Brunswick: Transaction Books.

Paulhus, D. L., & Williams, K. M. (2002). The dark triad of personality: Narcissism, Machiavellianism, and psychopathy. *Journal of Research in Personality*, 36(6), 556-563.

Péloquin, K., Lafontaine, M. F., & Brassard, A. (2011). A dyadic approach to the study of romantic attachment, dyadic empathy, and psychological partner aggression. *Journal of Social and Personal Relationships*, 28, 915-942.

Pennebaker, J. W. (1997). *Opening up: The healing power of expressing emotions*. New York: Guilford Press.

Petronio, S. (1991). Communication boundary management: A theoretical model of managing disclosure of private information between marital couples. *Communication Theory*, 4, 311-335.

Pistole, M. C. (1993). Attachment relationships: Self-disclosure and trust. *Journal of Mental Health Counseling, 15*, 94-106.

Pistole, M. C., Clark, E. M., & Tubbs, A. L. (1995). Love relationships: Attachment style and the investment model. *Journal of Mental Health Counseling, 17*, 199-209.

Planalp, S., & Honeycutt, J. M. (1985). Events that increase uncertainty in personal relationships. *Human Communication Research, 11*, 593-604.

Planalp, S., Rutherford, D. K., & Honeycutt, J. M. (1988). Events that increase uncertainty in personal relationships II replication and extension. *Human Communication Research, 14*(4), 516-547.

Reddy, V. (2008). *How infants know minds.* Boston: Harvard University Press.

Regan, P. C. (2008). *The mating game: A primer on love, sex, and marriage.* Thousand Oaks: SAGE Publications.

Reis, H. T., & Carothers, B. J. (2014). Black and white or shades of gray: Are gender differences categorical or dimensional? *Current Directions in Psychological Science, 23*(1), 19-26.

Reis, H. T., & Clark, M. S. (2013). Responsiveness. In J. A. Simpson & L. Campbell (Eds.), *Oxford handbook of close relationships* (pp. 400-423). New York: Oxford University Press.

Reis, H. T., & Shaver, P. (1988). Intimacy as an interpersonal process. *Handbook of Personal Relationships, 24*(3), 367-389.

Rempel, J. K., Holmes, J. G., & Zanna, M. P. (1985). Trust in close relationships. *Journal of Personality and Social Psychology, 49*(1), 95-112.

Rodriguez, N., & Ryave, A. (1990). Telling lies in everyday life: Motivational and organizational consequences of sequential preferences. *Qualitative Sociology, 13*, 195-210.

Roloff, M. E., & Cloven, D. H. (1994). When partners transgress: Maintaining violated relationships. In D. J. Canary & L. Stafford (Eds.), *Communication and relational maintenance* (pp. 23-43). San Diego, CA: Academic Press.

Roloff, M. E., Soule, K. P., & Carey, C. M. (2001). Reasons for remaining in a relationship and responses to relational transgressions. *Journal of Social and Personal Relationships, 18*(3), 362-385.

Rusbult, C. E. (1980). Commitment and satisfaction in romantic associations: A test of the investment model. *Journal of Experimental Social Psychology*, 16(2), 172-186.

Rusbult, C. E., Finkel, E. J., & Kumashiro, M. (2009). The Michelangelo phenomenon. *Current Directions in Psychological Science*, 18(6), 305-309.

Rusbult, C. E., Hannon, P. A., Stocker, S. L., & Finkel, E. J. (2005). Forgiveness and relational repair. In Worthington Jr, E. L. (Ed.), *Handbook of forgiveness* (pp. 185-205). New York: Routledge.

Rusbult, C. E., Olsen, N., Davis, J. L., & Hannon, P. (2001). Commitment and relationship maintenance mechanisms. In J. H. Harvey & A. Wenzel (Eds.), *Close romantic relationships: Maintenance and enhancement* (pp. 87-113). Mahwah, NJ: Lawrence Erlbaum Associates.

Rusbult, C. E., Verette, J., Whitney, G. A., Slovik, L. F., & Lipkus, I. (1991). Accommodation processes in close relationships: Theory and preliminary empirical evidence. *Journal of Personality and Social Psychology*, 60(1), 53-78.

Saarni, C., & Lewis, M. (1993). Deceit and illusion in human affairs. In C. Saarni & M. Lewis (Eds.), *Lying and deception in everyday life* (pp. 1-29). New York: Guilford Press.

Sagarin, B. J., Rhoads, K. V., & Cialdini, R. B. (1998). Deceiver's distrust: Denigration as a consequence of undiscovered deception. *Personality and Social Psychology Bulletin*, 24, 1167-1176.

Sarason, B. R., & Sarason, I. G. (2001). Ongoing aspects of relationships and health outcomes: Social support, social control, companionship, and relationship meaning. In J. Harvey & A. Wenzel (Eds.), *Close romantic relationships: Maintenance and enhancement* (pp. 227-298). Mahwah, NJ: Lawrence Erlbaum Associates.

Saxe, L. (1991). Lying: Thoughts of an applied social psychologist. *American Psychologist, 46*, 409-415.

Scher, S. J., & Darley, J. M. (1997). How effective are the things people say to apologize? Effects of the realization of the apology speech act. *Journal of Psycholinguistic Research*, 26, 127-140.

Selterman, D., & Koleva, S. (2015). Moral judgements of close relationship behaviors. *Journal of Social and Personal Relationships, 32,* 922-945.

Senchak, M., & Leonard, K. E. (1992). Attachment styles and marital adjustment among newlywed couples. *Journal of Social and Personal Relationships, 9,* 51-64.

Shaver, P., & Hazan, C. (1985). Incompatibility, loneliness, and "limerence." In W. Ickes (Ed.), *Compatible and incompatible relationships* (pp. 163-184). New York: Springer.

Shaver, P., & Hazan, C. (1987). Being lonely, falling in love: Perspectives from attachment theory. Special Issue: Loneliness: Theory, research, and applications. *Journal of Social Behavior and Personality, 2,* 105-124.

Shaver, P. R., Hazan, C., & Bradshaw, D. (1988). The integration of three behavioral systems. In R. J. Sternberg & M. L. Barnes (Eds.), *The psychology of love,* (pp. 68-99). New Haven, CT: Yale University Press.

Siegel, D. J. (2012). *Pocket guide to interpersonal neurobiology: An integrative handbook of the mind* (Norton Series on Interpersonal Neurobiology). New York: WW Norton & Company.

Sillars, A. L., Coletti, S. F., Parry, D., & Rogers, M. A. (1982). Coding verbal conflict tactics: Nonverbal and perceptual correlates of the "avoidance-distributive-integrative" distinction. *Human Communication Research, 9*(1), 83-95.

Simpson, J. A. (1990). Influence of attachment styles on romantic relationships. *Journal of Personality and Social Psychology, 59,* 971-980.

Simpson, J. A., & Belsky, J. (2008). Attachment theory within a modern evolutionary framework. In J. Cassidy & P. R. Shaver (Eds.), *Handbook of attachment: Theory, research and clinical applications* (pp. 131-157). New York: Guilford Press.

Simpson, J. A., Collins, W. A., & Salvatore, J. E. (2011). The impact of early interpersonal experience on adult romantic relationship functioning: Recent findings from the Minnesota longitudinal study of risk and adaptation. *Current Directions in Psychological Science, 20*(6), 355-359.

Simpson, J. A., Kim, J. S., Fillo, J., Ickes, W., Rholes, W. S., Oriña, M. M., & Winterheld, H. A. (2011). Attachment and the management of empathic accuracy in relationship-threatening situations. *Personality and Social Psychology Bulletin*, 37(2), 242-254.

Slotter, E. B., & Finkel, E. J. (2009). The strange case of sustained dedication to an unfulfilling relationship: Predicting commitment and breakup from attachment anxiety and need fulfillment within relationships. *Personality and Social Psychology Bulletin*, 35(1), 85-100.

Solomon, D. H., & Knobloch, L. K. (2004). A model of relational turbulence: The role of intimacy, relational uncertainty, and interference from partners in appraisals of irritations. *Journal of Social and Personal Relationships*, 21, 795-816.

Solomon, D. H., & Samp, J. A. (1998). Power and problem appraisal: Perceptual foundations of the chilling effect in dating relationships. *Journal of Social and Personal Relationships*, 15, 191-209.

Solomon, R. C. (1993). What a tangled web: Deception and self-deception in philosophy. In C. Saarni & M. Lewis (Eds.), *Lying and deception in everyday life* (pp. 30-58). New York: Guilford Press.

Spitzberg, B. H., & Cupach, W. R. (1994). Dark side denouement. In W. R., Cupach & B. H. Spitzberg (Eds.), *The dark side of interpersonal communication*, (pp. 315-320). Hillsdale, NJ: Lawrence Erlbaum Associates.

Sprecher, S. (2002). Sexual satisfaction in premarital relationships: Associations with satisfaction, love, commitment, and stability. *Journal of Sex Research*, 39, 190-196.

Sprecher, S., & Fehr, B. (2011). Dispositional attachment and relationship-specific attachment as predictors of compassionate love for a partner. *Journal of Social and Personal Relationships*, 28, 558-574.

Sprecher, S., & Regan, P. C. (1998). Passionate and companionate love in courting and young married couples. *Sociological Inquiry*, 68, 163-185.

Stafford, L., & Canary, D. J. (1991). Maintenance strategies and romantic relationship type, gender and relational characteristics. *Journal of Social and Personal Relationships*, 8, 217-242.

Stanley, S. M., & Markman, H. J. (1992). Assessing commitment in personal relationships. *Journal of Marriage and the Family*, 55, 595-608.

Stanley, S. M., Rhoades, G. K., & Markman, H. J. (2006). Sliding versus deciding: Inertia and the premarital cohabitation effect. *Family Relations*, 55, 499-509.

Stiff, J. B., Kim, H. J., & Ramesh, C. N. (1992). Truth biases and aroused suspicion in relational deception. *Communication Research*, 19, 326-345.

Swann Jr, W. B., & Gill, M. J. (1997). Confidence and accuracy in person perception: Do we know what we think we know about our relationship partners? *Journal of Personality and Social Psychology*, 73(4), 747-757.

Tangney, J. P., & Dearing, R. L. (2002). *Shame and guilt*. New York: Guilford Press.

Theiss, J. A., Knobloch, L. K., Checton, M. G., & Magsamen-Conrad, K. (2009). Relationship characteristics associated with the experience of hurt in romantic relationships: A test of the relational turbulence model. *Human Communication Research*, 35(4), 588-615.

Theiss, J. A., & Solomon, D. H. (2008). Parsing the mechanisms that increase relational intimacy: The effects of uncertainty amount, open communication about uncertainty, and the reduction of uncertainty. *Human Communication Research*, 34(4), 625-654.

Thibaut, J. W., & Kelley, H. H. (1959). *The social psychology of groups*. New York: Wiley.

Thomas, G, & Fletcher, G. J. O. (1997). Empathic accuracy in close relationships. In W. J. Ickes (Ed). *Empathetic accuracy*. (pp. 194-217). New York: Guilford Press.

Tice, D. M., Baumeister, R. F., & Zhang, L. (2004). The role of emotion in self-regulation: Differing roles of positive and negative emotion. In P. Philippot & R. S. Feldman (Eds.), *The regulation of emotion* (pp. 213-226). Mahwah, NJ: Lawrence Erlbaum Associates.

Trivers, R. L. (2011). *The folly of fools: The logic of deceit and self-deception in human life*. New York. Basic Books.

Tucker, P., & Aron, A. (1993). Passionate love and marital satisfaction at key transition points in the family life cycle. *Journal of Social and Clinical Psychology*, 12(2), 135-147.

Turner, R. E., Edgley, C., & Olmstead, G. (1975). Information control in conversations: Honesty is not always the best policy. *Kansas Journal of Sociology*, 11, 69-89.

Van Kleef, G. A. (2009). How emotions regulate social life the emotions as social information (EASI) model. *Current Directions in Psychological Science*, 18(3), 184-188.

Vaughan, D. (1986). *Uncoupling: Turning points in intimate relationships*. New York: Oxford University Press.

Vigil, J. M. (2009). A socio-relational framework of sex differences in the expression of emotion. *Behavioral and Brain Sciences*, 32(5), 375-390.

Waldron, V. R., & Kelley, D. L. (2005). Forgiving communication as a response to relational transgressions. *Journal of Social and Personal Relationships*, 22(6), 723-742.

Waters, E., Merrick, S., Treboux, D., Crowell, J., & Albersheim, L. (2000). Attachment security in infancy and early adulthood: A twenty-year longitudinal study. *Child Development*, 71, 684-689.

Weger Jr, H. (2006). Associations among romantic attachment, argumentativeness, and verbal aggressiveness in romantic relationships. *Argumentation and Advocacy*, 43, 29-40.

Wegner, D. M., Giuliano, T., & Hertel, P. (1985). Cognitive interdependence in close relationships. In W. J. Ickes (Ed.), *Compatible and incompatible relationships* (pp. 253-276). New York: Springer-Verlag.

Weinfield, N. S., Sroufe, L. A., Egeland, B., & Carlson, E. (2008). Individual differences in infant-caregiver attachment: Conceptual and empirical aspects of security. In J. Cassidy & P. R. Shaver (Eds.), *Handbook of attachment: Theory, research and clinical applications* (pp. 78-101). New York: Guilford Press.

Wieselquist, J. (2009). Interpersonal forgiveness, trust, and the investment model of commitment. *Journal of Social and Personal Relationships*, 26(4), 531-548.

Wilmot, W. W. (2002). Communication spirals, paradoxes, and conundrums. In J. Stewart (Ed.), *Bridges not walls: A book about interpersonal communication* (pp. 471-486). New York: McGraw-Hill Higher Education.

Wood, J. T. (2007). *Interpersonal Communication Everyday Encounters* (5th ed). Belmont, CA: Thomson Wadsworth.

Worthington, E. L., & Scherer, M. (2004). Forgiveness is an emotion-focused coping strategy that can reduce health risks and promote health resilience: Theory, review, and hypotheses. *Psychology & Health,* 19(3), 385-405.

Younger, J. W., Piferi, R. L., Jobe, R. L., & Lawler, K. A. (2004). Dimensions of forgiveness: The views of laypersons. *Journal of Social and Personal Relationships,* 21, 837-855.

Zech, E., Rimé, B., & Nils, F. (2004). Social sharing of emotion, emotional recovery, and interpersonal aspects. In P. Philippot & R. S. Feldman (Eds.), *The regulation of emotion* (pp. 157-185). Mahwah, NJ: Lawrence Erlbaum Associates.

Zeifman, D., & Hazan, C. (1997). Attachment: The bond in pair-bonds. In J. A. Simpson & T. K. Kenrick (Eds.), *Evolutionary social psychology* (pp. 237-263). Mahwah, NJ: Lawrence Erlbaum Associates.

Zeifman, D., & Hazan, C. (2008). Pair bonds as attachments: Re-evaluating the evidence. In J. Cassidy & P. R. Shaver (Eds.), *Handbook of attachment: Theory, research and clinical applications* (pp. 436-455). New York: Guilford Press.

About the Authors

Tim Cole, PhD, is an award-winning teacher and scholar. He is an associate professor in the College of Communication at DePaul University in Chicago where he does research and teaches classes on attachment, deception, and close relationships. Dr. Cole is an avid reader, runner, and dog lover.

Emily Duddleston earned a master's degree in relational communication from DePaul University, where she worked with Dr. Cole. She currently resides in Minneapolis, where she loves being with family and friends, going Up North, and exploring breweries.

91394637R10129

Made in the USA
San Bernardino, CA
21 October 2018